IN LOVE IN
NEW YORK

IN **LOVE** IN
NEW YORK

A Guide to the Most Romantic Destinations
in the Greatest City in the World

CAITLIN LEFFEL

and

JACOB LEHMAN

Rizzoli
ex libris

TO MY CONSTANTS: ALEX AND NEW YORK. —CL

TO JOANA, AND THE CITY WHERE I FOUND HER. —JL

CONTENTS

THE CITY THAT NEVER SLEEPS ALONE

I n 1977, Milton Glaser and Bobby Zarem created the iconic heart logo for New York. At the time the city was not quite looking or feeling her best. Unlike those venerable European queens of romance—Paris, Venice, Barcelona, London—New York was a young town with a comparatively short history of accelerated development. Her early marriage to Prosperity faltered after the Depression and the War, the breakup was long and hard, and by the 1970s she had been left unloved for far too long. While it's difficult now to believe that such a thing was necessary, the logo was commissioned by the New York State department of commerce to promote tourism, to lend a sense of warmth and romance to a city whose heart had grown so cool that no amount of love letters from Woody Allen, Truman Capote, or Stephen Sondheim could help it.

Almost forty years later, that perfect red heart is as much an emblem of New York as the skyline—and it's far from the only one. There are countless valentines to this great metropolis: Woody's New York is a mostly-uptown bounty of culture and wit, where gray days look as appealing as sunny ones; Joan Didion's, in *Goodbye to All That*, is a playground for the young and new, whose charm derives from—not in spite of—the city's hard edges; Nora Ephron refined the classic cinematic meet-cute all over Manhattan, from Katz's to the top of the Empire State Building; Jonathan Ames's *Bored to Death* characters are well-dressed and hyper-literate as they bumble endearingly around the boroughs in noble and misguided pursuits; while Sinatra's New York conjures up our dapper Yankees, at whose stadium his version of the song is played after every game. (And inspired the city's modern anthem by self-proclaimed "New Sinatra" Jay-Z, which describes the city as a "concrete jungle where dreams are made.") These few examples among countless show that New York is perfectly imperfect, worthy of undying affection, and dazzling enough to inspire an entire genre of famous love notes.

Whether you're new to your relationship, new to the city, or an old pro at both, New York is there to seduce, excite, console, and entertain. For many the city is a destination, whether for a vacation of indulgent shopping, a romantic break, a honeymoon, or even a wedding. For millions more for whom the city is already home, it's a place that continues to seduce no matter how long you've lived here, the setting for myriad famous literary and celluloid love stories, and for countless more which might never make it to page or screen. The purpose of this book is dual: it guides you through the various stages of a New York–themed courtship, offering suggestions on what to see, do, eat, and visit with a lover. But it also inspires a couple to fall head-over-heels for this city—or rekindle the romance with it you once had but which has dulled over time.

As if to follow the most romantic tourist's itinerary, we begin with New York's first impressions, those iconic invitations the city extends to potential suitors around the world. From breathtaking views of the skyline to blissful afternoons paddling rowboats in the park, and from the dining rooms of the finest restaurants to the rooftops and balconies of lovers' landmarks, these are the beloved grand gestures that are for visitors to New York what a bouquet of red roses might be for a lover on a first date. From there we spend time getting to know the city a little better, taking a romantic tour of its most charming and seductive neighborhoods and singling out the sweetest spots and most engaging distractions to be found in each—whether it's a visit to Chelsea's gallery district or drinks on the Brooklyn waterfront. In the third chapter we hone in on specific suggestions for dates and romantic evenings to suit every interest and mood, from picnics in the city's many beautiful parks to ideas for putting a local twist on the classic dinner-and-a-movie date. From there we take you out of the heart of the city itself with romantic excursions into the beautiful countryside that surrounds New York, from the lush vineyards of the North Fork to the stunning Hudson River Valley and the soft sands of the Hamptons' beaches. And finally, for those who've decided that New York is where their heart belongs, we present a careful guide to getting married in the city, with recommendations for everything from the perfect locations for a ceremony to shopping for dresses for the big day.

While we've put together a mosaic of the romantic, the intimate, the classic, and the sexy parts of the city, we also encourage you to discover your own reasons to love New York, by keeping your eyes open and your feet on the pavement. The pleasures of the city entice at every turn: autumn leaves in Central Park; getting lost in the West Village; the first glimpse of the illuminated skyline from your cab coming in from the airport, beckoning you hither. There is romance on every corner of every street of every borough of this city. Let's find it.

CHAPTER 1

LOVE AT FIRST SIGHT

"**A** town that existed in black and white pulsating to the great tunes of George Gershwin"—this is one of the descriptions Woody Allen's Isaac Davis uses for New York during the glorious opening montage of *Manhattan*. Indeed, part of the charm of this city is how quickly it turns from a maddening crush of people and noise into a captivating movie moment, with full orchestra in the background. This is a place of grand, impressive gestures, the types from which great love affairs are born: front-row seats at grand spectacles of culture; seductive intimacy at classic haunts from literature and film; and breathtaking views from skyscrapers, bridges, and parks.

As with any kind of romance, falling in love with New York requires first your seeing the city at its very best. In this chapter, we present the city's biggest and brightest stars—the classics that are beloved for a reason. All you and your lover need to do is mentally supply the Gershwin—or your preferred Big Apple love theme—and let the city sweep you off your feet.

FIRST IMPRESSIONS

Do you believe in love at first sight? As New Yorkers, we've heard scores of stories about people's first impressions of the city—not necessarily the first thing they saw when they got off of the plane or train or out of the car, but their first glimpse of one of the city's iconic, unique, and breathtaking panoramas that instantly quickens the pulse and makes you fall in love with New York.

Whether you and your sweetheart are visiting the city for the first time, are in and out regularly, or make your home here, those first impressions are views you will continue to go back to. They are the sparks that keep your romance with the city—and each other—going, the original and unchanging beauty marks that make New York the romantic icon that it is. These outstanding, only-in-New-York images imprint the city's grandeur in your brain and set the stage for the seduction, the secrets, and the affection that will follow.

The view of Manhattan at night while traveling in a cab from Queens

For many visitors, their love affair with the city starts in the cab from the airport. When driving west into Manhattan from JFK or LaGuardia, suggest that your driver take one of the bridges rather than the Queens–Midtown Tunnel. In addition to saving money on the toll, you'll both be in for a treat as your car slowly climbs out of the maze of highways and begins to cross the water. The view from the bridges is one of the best places to see the classic—and justifiably famous—New York City skyline, and this iconic vista always feels at once familiar and brand-new. This sight is particularly glorious at night, appearing as NYC's brilliant, electrical welcome mat that she lays out for each and every visitor.

See the city from the top of the Empire State Building

A must for every tourist, a trip to the top of the Empire State Building is a particularly special journey for a couple in love, having served as the setting for dramatic romantic reunions in such classic films as *An Affair to Remember*, *Sleepless in Seattle*, and *King Kong* (which offers either a tragic end to a misunderstood love or a joyful union of hero and heroine, depending on whose side you're on). Even if you have visited the ESB before, it's worth another trip as the building nears the end of a historic green renovation. The $550 million renovation, undertaken with the Clinton Climate Initiative, will cut the building's energy use by 38 percent and showcase the Empire State Building as a premier example for the city—and the world—of how new green building practices can be implemented in older buildings. Refurbishments include a renovated lobby with streamlined queuing for visitors, smart elevators that use time- and energy-efficient technology to reduce wait times and energy usage, reproductions of damaged art deco murals that were covered up in the 1960s, and new exhibits on the 2nd and 80th floors about sustainability and construction. Of course, lovebirds may just be interested in racing up to the top for a kiss under the evening stars. If that's the case, you'd be wise to purchase your observatory tickets in advance online—and don't forget to check the calendar on the ESB's website, which tells you what colors the three layers of lights will be each night and what they stand for. If you're planning to pop the question up there, keep in mind that there is live music on the 86th floor observation deck Thursday, Friday, and Saturday nights, and the musicians do take requests for special songs. As for weddings, the only way to make the ESB the site of your nuptials is to enter their annual Valentine's Day wedding contest. Entrants must submit a two-minute video detailing their love story via any of the ESB's social-media channels; three

couples win a Valentine's Day wedding (or vow renewal) on the observation deck. *The Empire State Building has two observation decks, on the 86th and 102nd floors. Tickets for both can be purchased online on the Empire State Building website or in the building's lobby upon arrival. The observation decks are open every day, rain or shine, from 8:00 a.m. to 2:00 a.m. (The last elevator up is at 1:15 a.m.) The current lighting schedule is also available online. 350 Fifth Avenue, between West 33rd and 34th Streets, in Manhattan. 212-736-3100. www.esbnyc.com. Subway: B, D, F, M, N, Q, R to 34th Street–Herald Square; 6 to 33rd Street.*

Take someone for a spin around the Top of the Rock

Rockefeller Center is one of the true icons of midtown Manhattan, and aside from its status as a historic landmark and one of the city's finest examples of art deco architecture, it's also home to some of the most romantic spots in town. If you've passed a winter in New York, you'll be familiar with the whimsy of its ice rink (*see page 28*); if you've passed a lifetime here, you might have memories of the Rainbow Room, the dazzling dinner and dance club on the 65th floor that's been the backdrop for more proposals than a Venetian gondola. After changing hands and closing for a period of major restoration, the landmarked interiors of the Rainbow Room were reopened in 2014, and just a few floors above it, the panoramas of the Top of the Rock beckon visitors to another of the city's finest elevated experiences. The roof of 30 Rockefeller Plaza, renovated and reopened to the public in 2005, affords unob-structed panoramic views of the city in each direction and manages to take in what even the Empire State Building cannot: the timeless silhouette of the ESB herself. Beautiful year-round and brilliant as a fireworks display at night, the views of the city from up here—the colors of Central Park to the north, the rivers to the east and west, and the needles of the Empire State and the Chrysler buildings flickering like candles a few blocks south—are breathtaking. Brave romantics should bring someone special on a clear evening and slow-dance around the roof deck, with the greatest city in the world beneath your feet. *Top of the Rock is open seven days a week from 8:00 a.m. to midnight. (The last elevator up is at 11:00 p.m.) Tickets are available online or in person at the ticket office. Rockefeller Center, between West 48th and 51st Streets and Fifth and Sixth Avenues, in Manhattan. 212-698-2000. www.topoftherockp.com. Subway: B, D, F, M to 47th–50th Streets–Rockefeller Center.*

Enjoy the view from the roof of the Metropolitan Museum of Art . . .

The roof of the city's premier cultural institution is also a seasonal sculpture garden that showcases the work of a different contemporary artist each year (past exhibitions

The Empire State Building and the New Yorker Hotel at night

have included a collection of three bright-colored balloon-animal sculptures by Jeff Koons and a continually evolving, environmentally sensitive bamboo structure by Doug and Mike Starn). But an equally good reason to make the trip up to the top of the building is the grand view of Central Park, which reveals the breathtaking magnitude of Calvert Vaux and Frederick Law Olmsted's gift to the city. In the spring and summer, the park is a rich, green carpet of trees, flanked by the ornate and stately buildings of the city's fanciest neighborhoods; in the fall, the green becomes flecked with gold, rust, and red. Drink in the view while the two of you sip lattes or cocktails from the Met's rooftop bar, and marvel at the lushness before your eyes. *The Metropolitan Museum of Art is open seven days a week, Sunday through Thursday from 10:00 a.m. to 5:30 p.m. and Friday and Saturday from 10:00 a.m. to 9:00 p.m. The Iris and B. Gerald Cantor Roof Garden is open seasonally from May through late fall during museum hours, weather permitting. 1000 Fifth Avenue, between East 80th and 84th Streets, in Manhattan. 212-535-7710. www.metmuseum.org. Subway: 4, 5, 6 to 86th Street.*

. . . or from the Temple of Dendur in the Sackler Wing

The Temple of Dendur is one of the Met's most iconic and beloved attractions, in part because of its breathtaking setting in a room with a high glass ceiling and a sloping glass wall, which looks onto a quiet, tree-lined nook of the park. The temple, which dates back to 15 BCE, was a gift to the United States from the Egyptian government in 1965, and in 1967, the Met won out over other institutional suitors to house it. The temple was re-erected in a specially designed room in the Sackler Wing, and it sits over a reflecting pool, which symbolizes the River Nile. The floor-to-ceiling glass wall on one side of the gallery provides a stunning backdrop to this incredible artifact, and the view of the park is particularly lovely during fall foliage—a view indelibly depicted in the famous "pepper" scene in *When Harry Met Sally. The Temple of Dendur is located in the museum's Sackler Wing and open during normal museum hours.*

Walk across the Brooklyn Bridge at dusk

Strolling along the wooden walkway of the Brooklyn Bridge is another one of the city's great classics, offering equal doses of history, sweeping views, and iconic experiences. Pick a time in summer when the nights are long, and start your walk while the sun is going down. By then, the hustle-bustle of the 130-year-old bridge's main job (shuttling citizens between Manhattan and Brooklyn) will be dying down, and the pedestrian walkway will be less crowded than it is on weekend days and early evenings. If you start your walk on the Manhattan side, don't forget to turn around

The Temple of Dendur at the Metropolitan Museum of Art

and enjoy the skyline views that the bridge graciously offers. The Brooklyn side of the bridge is conveniently located near the lovely new Brooklyn Bridge Park, where you can continue to take in the view of our breathtaking skyline from a bench along the water. *The Manhattan side of the bridge starts at City Hall (Subway: 4, 5, 6 to Brooklyn Bridge–City Hall), and the Brooklyn side of the bridge starts at Adams and Tillary Streets (Subway: A, C to High Street).*

See the sunset from the tip of Manhattan at Wagner Park . . .

On the southern end of Manhattan, near historic Battery Park and the epicenter of the downtown tourism scene, Robert F. Wagner Jr. Park somehow manages to remain an underappreciated vantage point along the city's riverbank. Wagner is the southernmost in a series of interconnected green spaces that define the perimeter of Battery Park City, a quiet, mostly residential neighborhood that borders the Financial District. The park's large, delicately sloping lawns face out across New York Harbor, offering a view that takes in everything from Governors Island and Staten Island to the Statue of Liberty, Ellis Island, and the waterfront of Jersey City across the Hudson River. In the early morning, the view from here is a glimpse of New York industry, with tugs, ferries, and barges busying the waterways. By evening, the scene is more tranquil, with less movement on the water and the lowering light of the sun beginning to sparkle on the surface. The large pink stone pavilion allows you to climb up for a better view, and it also houses a popular high-end Italian restaurant—Gigino—where you and your partner can sit for a glass of wine or a meal overlooking the water. (It's the perfect place to relax after an afternoon seeing the downtown sights—or to avoid the crowds yet to see them.) Those looking for simpler pleasures should pick a spot on the grass and watch the sunset turn New Jersey and Lady Liberty into silhouettes, while the noise of the city softly echoes behind you. *Robert F. Wagner Jr. Park, between the Hudson River Esplanade and Battery Place, in Manhattan. Call for hours. 212-528-2228. www.gigino-wagnerpark.com. Subway: 4, 5 to Bowling Green; R to Whitehall Street–South Ferry; 1 to South Ferry. Gigino's, 20 Battery Place at the Esplanade.*

. . . or from the Boat Basin Café on the Upper West Side

Perched at the western edge of the city at West 79th Street, a welcome interruption to the serene ascent of Riverside Park along the Hudson River, the Boat Basin Café is *the* classic seasonal haunt of the Upper West Side. Open from the first sign of a daffodil in spring to the drop of the last leaf in fall (or roughly from March through

October every year), the café offers the simplest pleasures of the warmer seasons: cold beer, barbecue, and a beautiful view out over the water. With checkered tablecloths, plastic tumblers for the drinks, and paper plates for the burgers and salads, this isn't one of the city's fancier venues. But the mood is always relaxed, and not even the celebratory crowds that congregate here on a busy night can interfere with its greatest attraction: seeing the sun dip slowly down across the river. As you move uptown, the Hudson River broadens and the landscape of New Jersey opposite rises from the lower industrial skylines of Jersey City and Hoboken into the grand green and gray facades of the Palisades. Whether you're in the charming covered circular room or facing the elements on the patio outside, the colors of the evening sun flood every corner of the café, and over the course of an evening the light can change from bright golden sunshine to the pinks and oranges of sunset to glowing moonlight. *The Boat Basin Café is open seasonally, March through October, seven days a week. Hours vary by day. West 79th Street and the Hudson River, in Manhattan. 212-496-5542. www.boatbasincafe.com. Subway: 1 to 79th Street.*

See the skyline from the Brooklyn Heights Promenade

The skyline of Manhattan remains one of New York's most recognizable and seductive features, its eccentric form written across the horizon with the flourish of a lover's autograph. Seen from any angle (even from within it), the skyline is a romantic sight for its grandeur alone. But seen from the promenade, a hallowed boardwalk that runs along the waterside edge of Brooklyn Heights, it is particularly so. One of Brooklyn's oldest and most beautiful neighborhoods, Brooklyn Heights grew up more than a century ago to accommodate the city's first commuters, the well-to-do workers of Wall Street who sought a peaceful retreat from the city's bustle. The promenade runs along the edge of the borough between Remsen and Orange Streets, overlooking a stretch of the East River and New York Harbor that divides Brooklyn from the eccentric mix of old towers and new glass skyscrapers that make up the Financial District. Positioned above the Brooklyn–Queens Expressway, neatly hiding the highway and somewhat dampening its noise, the boardwalk is lined with benches and balustrades for romantic reflection along the way. With some of the city's prettiest tree-lined streets of brownstones behind you and a postcard view of lower Manhattan and the Brooklyn and Manhattan Bridges in front, the promenade is an ideal place for a romantic walk at any time, in any season. *Above the BQE between Remsen and Orange Streets, in Brooklyn. www.nyharborparks.org/visit/brhe.html. Subway: A, C to High Street; 2, 3 to Clark Street; R to Court Street.*

CLASSICS

"He was too romantic about Manhattan," continues Allen's character, in the greatest tribute to the city on celluloid. He goes on to correct himself—"No, no—corny, too corny for a man of my taste"—before Gershwin booms in again and the soaring sight of the skyline at night takes our breath away. In New York, and in the name of love, can there ever be such a thing as romantic overstatement?

Every great metropolis likes to consider itself a backdrop for romance, and, according to most travel guides at least, has any number of legendarily seductive locations in which amorous visitors can set their own romantic comedies. Venice has San Marco and the Grand Canal; Paris, the Eiffel Tower and Montmartre; London, Covent Garden and the Serpentine. But as you come to know a city, you can stray with more confidence from the beaten paths and explore the place with more sophistication. In Venice, you might find yourself getting blissfully lost in the backstreet canals; in Paris, seeing a classic movie in one of the great old art deco theaters; or in London, discovering one of the many hidden wine bars down by the Thames.

One of the marvelous things about New York is that here the lines are blurred between high and low, between tourist and local, between pretentious and authentic. Certainly there are the star attractions, the icons (like those described in "First Impressions," see pages 14–21) that decorate guidebooks and justifiably draw visitors in droves, like moths to their monumental flames. And of course there are myriad lesser-known distractions that occupy more locals than tourists. But with a range of grand gestures that are at once iconic and accessible, New York is unique in being a perfect playground for romantics new and familiar. It is this kind of duality that inspired Joan Didion to call the city "the mysterious nexus of all love," and to write that "to think of 'living' there [in New York] was to reduce the miraculous to the mundane." There are things to do here that in lesser cities might be the very peak of extravagant cliché—but which, in the context of New York, are simply great and gloriously romantic.

Champagne on the balcony at Lincoln Center

Few of New York's grand old institutions are as wonderful as the Metropolitan Opera. Few of the opera's pleasures are as eagerly anticipated as the first sip of chilled champagne at intermission, and the chance to fortify oneself for the inevitable tragedy of the final acts. And there can be few places on Earth, let alone in the city, where you can enjoy these things looking out over something as beautiful as Lincoln Center's

The entrance to the Metropolitan Opera at Lincoln Center

plaza. Gently lit by night and populated solely by passionate and well-dressed consumers of the city's finest culture, the plaza is a haven of old-fashioned and high-end romance, where tuxedoed gentlemen and elaborately gowned ladies gather in season for concerts, ballets, and operas. Taking in the scene from the balcony of the opera house is as romantic and as uniquely New York as anything Woody could ever conjure up for Diane. *Lincoln Center Josie Robertson Plaza, Columbus Avenue between West 62nd and 65th Streets, in Manhattan. 212-875-5456. www.lincolncenter.org. Subway: 1 to 66th Street–Lincoln Center.*

Breakfast at Balthazar

Who says romance only happens at night? Candlelit dinners and moonlit drinks have their place, but breakfast at Balthazar is one of New York's most surprising romantic gestures. Balthazar was opened in the heart of SoHo by the culinary impresario Keith McNally in 1997, and in little more than fifteen years has become an institution on par with any celebrated restaurant in the city. Its tables are packed (with as many locals as tourists) for every brunch, lunch, and dinner service throughout the year, making a reservation hard to come by. But in the early weekday mornings, while most tourists are mastering the subway map and New Yorkers are pushing past them on the way to work, this majestic bistro is a quiet oasis of old-school formality and European charm. Find yourself a table facing the windows onto Spring Street, order a pot of coffee and a basket of delicate pastries, and you'll have all the romance of a quiet Parisian morning in the heart of New York City. *Balthazar is open seven days week. Hours vary by day. 80 Spring Street, between Broadway and Crosby Street, in Manhattan. 212-965-1414. www.balthazarny. com. Subway: 6 to Spring Street; N, R to Prince Street; B, D, F, M to Broadway–Lafayette Street.*

An afternoon in the rowboats on the lake in Central Park

Rowing on the lake in Central Park is one of the city's best-known lovebird attractions that still manages to charm the socks off of visitors, despite its popularity. As you float past the Loeb Boathouse, you'll find your boat drifting away from the peopled drives and pathways into a wild wonderland of trees, birdlife, and the beautiful Bow Bridge, exactly as Olmsted and Vaux intended. Even when the park is teeming with visitors, boating on the lake feels calm and intimate, a completely private date in the middle of the most vibrant city in the world. *Rowboats are available to rent April through November, at the Loeb Boathouse, West 75th Street near Fifth Avenue, in Manhattan. 212-517-2233. www.thecentralparkboathouse.com. Subway: 6 to 68th Street–Hunter College; B, C to 72nd Street; N, Q, R to Fifth Avenue–59th Street.*

An evening at the Carlyle

The Carlyle Hotel has been a retreat—and a hideout—for the high-society set since the 1940s; in 2000, it was called "a palace of secrets" by the *New York Times*. Equally famous for luxuriousness and discretion, the Carlyle for decades was a natural home away from home for the rich and famous, and unofficial city lore has the Carlyle as the setting of many unconfirmed liaisons, including, most famously, the story of how Marilyn Monroe was shuttled through secret underground passages to President John F. Kennedy's private suite. An aura of seduction and intimacy prevails, and if you can't afford to stay there (rooms start at around $500 per night), there are other ways to experience one of the most classically romantic settings in the city. The hotel has had an enduring connection with music and performance since it opened (the

A rowboat on the lake in front of Bow Bridge in Central Park

composer Richard Rodgers arrived as the hotel's first tenant), and today, there are two venues in the hotel that offer several weekly live acts. Café Carlyle is the supper club where Woody Allen famously has a regular Monday night jazz gig; the venue operates cabaret-style, with dinner served during performances in a lovely room featuring murals painted by the art director of the 1952 film *Moulin Rouge*. Bemelmans Bar is more casual (*casual* being a relative term here), with live music every night. *Reservations recommended for all performances. Visit the hotel's website for information on upcoming performers and performances. 35 East 76th Street at Madison Avenue, in Manhattan. 212-744-1600. www.thecarlyle.com. Subway: 6 to 77th Street.*

Walk down Cherry Esplanade in the Brooklyn Botanic Garden

Situated alongside Prospect Park, the sprawling sibling of Central Park that Olmsted and Vaux designed after completing the latter, is the Brooklyn Botanic Garden. Picturesque, classically landscaped, and big enough to feel surprisingly quiet throughout the year, the botanic garden is one of the most romantic spots in the borough, a pastoral paradise where couples can discover quiet clearings within fields of luxuriant flowers, secret spots alongside ponds and lakes, and benches hidden under the branches of weeping willows. A stroll around all of the gardens can be seductive, from the formal display of the roses to the olfactory pleasures of the Fragrance Garden. But once a year, in the late spring, the garden's collection of cherry trees blossom in unison, transforming part of the park with a flood of delicate scents and colors. Walk down the allées of Cherry Esplanade in season, and it's as if the park was designed just for you, with soft petals covering the grass underfoot like a blanket of confetti, and the trees' elderly branches letting sunlight through a lacelike canopy overhead. *Cherry blossom season usually peaks at the end of April; follow the garden's CherryWatch online for details. The Brooklyn Botanic Garden is open Tuesday through Sunday, year-round. Hours vary depending on the season. 150 Eastern Parkway between Underhill and Washington Avenues, in Brooklyn. 718-623-7200. www.bbg.org. Subway: 2, 3 to Eastern Parkway–Brooklyn Museum.*

Dinner at La Grenouille

In the winter of 2012, La Grenouille celebrated its fiftieth anniversary. Famous for its excessive displays of fresh flowers, which grew from the table roses of opening night in 1962 to the vast bouquets that decorate the walls today, La Grenouille is a blast from New York's past, a bastion of French haute cuisine in the kind of lavish modern setting that simply no longer exists elsewhere in the city (and in very few places the world over). Formal dress is required—and once you're seated at a heavily adorned

The Cherry Esplanade at the Brooklyn Botanic Garden

table, equipped with its own lamp with tasseled shade and in view of the rest of the elegantly lit dining room, you'll understand why. With an elaborate, classic French menu—featuring many dishes, from the delicate grilled Dover sole to the celebrated cheese soufflé, that have endured through decades—and a wine list to tempt even the best-behaved wallet, dinner here is an exercise in indulgence. For anyone whose romantic ideas of New York are rooted in the fictions of *Barefoot in the Park* or Woody Allen movies, dinner at La Grenouille is an escape to fantasy—and the food is almost too good to be real. *La Grenouille is open Tuesday through Saturday, for lunch from 12:00 p.m. to 2:30 p.m. and dinner from 5:00 p.m. to 10:30 p.m. 3 East 52nd Street between Fifth and Madison Avenues, in Manhattan. 212-752-1495. www.la-grenouille.com. Subway: E, M to Fifth Avenue–53rd Street; B, D, E to Seventh Avenue; 6 to 51st Street; F to 57th Street.*

Take to the ice

Unlike swimming, badminton, or track, ice-skating is unique in being the only sporting adventure of one's youth that is happily reinvented in later life as a romantic pastime par excellence. Taking a date—or even the long-standing love of your life—to one of New York's ice rinks after dark can be one of the most enjoyable and romantic experiences to be had in the city. Rinks open up all around the five boroughs in winter, but three that stand out as the best examples of their kind are the Wollman in Central Park, the Rink at Rockefeller Center, and the Plaza at the Standard Hotel by the High Line. Skating at the Standard means taking on a very cool crowd of fashionable tourists and slick locals at a seductively lit rink amid the bustling nightlife of the Meatpacking District. There's a touch of European civility in the alpine-style café next door, where exhilarated skaters can warm themselves with suitable snacks, from hot chocolate and pretzels to cocktails and mulled wine. Further north in midtown, the Rink at Rockefeller Center is the city's most picturesque piece of ice, and it draws the biggest crowds as a result. Set at the foot of 30 Rockefeller Plaza, beneath the glittering lights of the biggest Christmas tree in town, the ice rink here is worth the inevitable wait, if only for the surreal vision of the majesty of midtown revolving around you. But nothing can quite rival a night at Wollman Rink, the pride of Central Park, where the ice seems to reflect the moonlight in the near darkness of the landscape around it, and where the windows and streetlamps of the city flicker beyond and the stars twinkle above. A tradition for New Yorkers from every corner of the city, a night at Wollman will make you see the park—and the city—in a whole new light. **Wollman Rink:** *Central Park, close to the West 59th Street and Sixth Avenue entrance, in Manhattan. www.wollmanskatingrink.com.*

Subway: N, Q, R to Fifth Avenue–59th Street; F to 57th Street; 1, A, B, C, D to 59th Street–Columbus Circle. **The Rink at Rockefeller Center:** *Fifth Avenue between West 49th and 50th Streets, in Manhattan. www.therinkatrockcenter.com. Subway: B, D, F, M to 47th–50th Streets–Rockefeller Center.* **The Standard Plaza:** *Washington Street at Little West 12th Street, in Manhattan. www.standardhotels.com/high-line/food-drink/the-standard-plaza. Subway: L to Eighth Avenue; A, C, E to 14th Street.*

A Red Snapper at the King Cole Bar and Salon

This classic New York cocktail spot off the lobby of the swank St. Regis Hotel takes its name from the expansive three-paneled Maxfield Parrish mural of merry Old King Cole and his fiddlers three that is displayed behind the elegant wood bar. Commissioned in 1906 by tycoon John Jacob Astor IV, the mural made its way to the St. Regis in 1932. And although it wasn't until 1950 that women were permitted in the bar, it quickly became a spot for high-society rendezvous; indeed, the St. Regis was a place of residence for at least two famous couples: Marilyn Monroe and Joe DiMaggio, and John Lennon and Yoko Ono (before they moved to the Dakota). Play your cards right, and you may be able to coax out of the bartender a secret of the mural that is much less elegant than the setting it hangs in. The Bloody Mary is the King Cole's signature drink, but those in the know will order it as a Red Snapper, which was what it was called when a St. Regis bartender in Paris introduced his vodka-and-tomato-juice concoction to the bar's clientele in the 1930s. This is the perfect nook to escape to after a stroll in Central Park, a movie at the Paris Theatre, or an afternoon of shopping at Bergdorf's, Bendel's, Tiffany's, or Harry Winston. *The King Cole Bar and Salon at the St. Regis Hotel is open daily. 2 East 55th Street between Madison and Fifth Avenues, in Manhattan. 212-339-6857. www.kingcolebar.com. Subway: N, Q, R to Fifth Avenue–59th Street; E, M to Fifth Avenue–53rd Street.*

Gelato in the Sculpture Garden at the Museum of Modern Art

New York's museums boast an embarrassment of riches, even beyond the art and artifacts they hold within their walls. The Abby Aldrich Rockefeller Sculpture Garden at MoMA is an enclosed street-level oasis from the hustle-bustle of midtown that is now one of the city's most appealing—yet still somewhat private—social spaces. Designed by the architect Philip Johnson in 1953, it has been the heart of the museum since 2004, when a renovation to the building by architect Yoshio Taniguchi revived the garden and repositioned the layout so it's on full display to all museumgoers as they enter the collections. The garden has examples from the museum's expansive repertoire, naturally, and a soothing reflecting pool, and it invites guests to do all the things you're not allowed to do in a museum hall. Here, you can wander on your own path, chat and laugh and drink and eat, or linger in the black Harry Bertoia chairs, which can be pushed together in a grouping of your own design. The Garden Bar offers gelato from beloved local purveyor **Il Laboratorio del Gelato** (*see page 79*), as well as coffee and drinks. The sculpture garden is open during museum hours, as well as during other special events, including an annual concert series in July. *The Abby Aldrich Rockefeller Sculpture Garden at the Museum of Modern Art is open year-round during museum hours, with free admission before the museum opens from 9:00 a.m. to 10:15 a.m. During regular museum hours, admission must be purchased to access the garden. 11 West 53rd Street between Fifth and Sixth Avenues, in Manhattan. 212-708-9400. www.moma.org. Subway: E, M to Fifth Avenue–53rd Street.*

A picnic and a movie in Bryant Park

Now more than twenty years old, the Bryant Park Summer Film Festival has become a NYC Monday-night summer tradition. Though other parks around the city have also started staging outdoor film festivals of their own, Bryant Park's free festival (which runs for ten weeks from June through August) is still the most popular, and in many ways still the best. One reason is the lineup, which focuses on the classics—typically a mix of Hitchcock, Hepburn (Audrey and Katharine), Redford, and Newman. Another reason is the boisterous, giddy excitement of attendees charging onto the lawn with their blankets at 5:00 p.m. The films start at sunset (between 8:00 and 9:00 p.m.), but come early with a blanket and your beloved to claim a space and enjoy a few hours lounging on the grass in this great midtown oasis. You can bring your own picnic or order in advance from the outpost of 'wichcraft at the park's northwestern corner. *The Bryant Park Summer Film Festival shows a movie every Monday evening for ten weeks starting in June. The film starts thirty minutes after sunset, and the lineup is announced in mid-May. Bryant Park is located between West 40th and 42nd Streets and between Fifth and Sixth Avenues, in Manhattan. www.bryantpark.org. Subway: B, D, F, M to 42nd Street–Bryant Park; 7 to Fifth Avenue–Bryant Park. 'wichcraft is located in the northwest corner of the park at West 42nd Street and Sixth Avenue, in Manhattan. To place a picnic order, call 212-780-0577 or order online at www.wichcraftnyc.com.*

Share a hot chocolate and a pretzel croissant at City Bakery

In 1990, before greenmarkets had replaced hot dog vendors as the city's most ubiqui-tous outdoor food source, a bakery and fresh food hall opened in the Flatiron District, and the city instantly fell in love. Within the walls of its original space, City Bakery has developed two signature items that are the new classics of native cuisine: the pretzel croissant and City Bakery hot chocolate. The croissant deliciously exemplifies the entrepreneurial melting pot of the city, marrying our beloved street-vendor pretzel with the French pastry skills that owner Maury Rubin brought back from his training in Paris. Pair this with two cups of City Bakery's luscious hot chocolate, and you have a cozy treat that's worth braving the snow for. People skeptical of chocolate's aphrodisiac powers will have their minds blown once they try a small sip of this dense, decadent treat. Perennially topping lists of the city's best cocoa spots ("What Katz's is to pastrami, City Bakery is to hot chocolate," *New York Magazine* proclaimed), City Bakery's hot chocolate is best enjoyed in a modest four-ounce pour, topped with a homemade marshmallow. In February, the bakery puts on a Hot Chocolate Festival featuring a different specialty flavor every day (such as ginger, espresso, pistachio, malted milk, rum raisin, and a special "love potion" on Valentine's Day), but the classic version is available year-round. *City Bakery is open seven days a week. 3 West 18th Street, between Fifth and Sixth Avenues, in Manhattan. 212-366-2414. www.citybakery.com. Subway: 4, 5, 6, L, N, Q, R to 14th Street–Union Square; F, M to 14th Street.*

CENTRAL PARK THROUGH THE SEASONS

Of all the city's treasures, Central Park—or just "the park," to its doting aficionados—is the truest emblem of romance in New York. The setting for countless love songs and romantic scenes on the silver screen, it's here that Sinatra sang of carving initials into bark, and here that Kermit and Miss Piggy enjoy their happiest moments in *The Muppets Take Manhattan*. But the park is also an indispensable part of Manhattan life, making it both the picturesque backdrop to millions of potential lovers' lives and an iconic romantic legend in its own right. Everybody who lives in New York has a favorite time of year to be in the park—some so much so that they can only conceive of being married here in that season (*see chapter 5*)—but each season brings its own unique charm to the most romantic 843 acres in the world.

FALL

"Lovers that bless the dark/on benches in Central Park/greet autumn in New York." So go the lyrics of Vernon Duke's melancholic ode to the city's fleeting embrace of this beautiful season. Every year, while tourists head upstate to marvel at the foliage

alongside the Hudson and as far north as the Adirondacks, New York couples need only travel as far as the park to surround themselves with color and feel their emotions enhanced by the delicate melancholy of fall. Of course, all of Central Park is a pleasure to explore throughout autumn, when its rich greens fade into yellows and reds and leaves crackle underfoot. But the mall—the only straight avenue in the park, located centrally a few blocks north of West 59th Street—is worth a few visits over the course of the season. Designed as a formal promenade along the lines of those in European parks of similar scale, the mall is lined with benches and overhung with rows of giant American elms, whose arcing green canopies shade the path from the sun in the summer. As the seasons change, the leaves of the elms move through a muddy spectrum of burnt oranges to an extraordinary yellow, and for a week or two before the onset of winter, the avenue glows from the light shining through them and the tarmac itself is softened with a rust-colored fabric of fallen leaves. There's nothing like it in the city. *The Central Park Mall is located in the middle of the park between West 66th and 72nd Streets, in Manhattan. Subway: N, Q, R to Fifth Avenue–59th Street; F to 57th Street.*

WINTER

After a snowstorm hits the city, make haste to Central Park, which becomes our version of a winter wonderland. While elsewhere in the city, powdery flakes quickly turn into gray slush, here delightful piles of picturesque white snow can gleam under the brilliant winter sun for days. Pick up a plastic sled en route (delis and bodegas near the park are usually stocked with cheap ones) and treat yourselves to a date with the pure pleasure of childhood as you zip down the park's little hills with dozens of the city's kids and kids at heart. The two most popular places to sled in the park are Pilgrim Hill, the park's black diamond of sledding, and Cedar Hill, which might be considered the bunny slope. But there are also plenty of small hills around the park that offer a less bustling, more intimate sledding experience. Or try your hand at making a snowman together, and admire the diverse crew of bulgy white snowmen that others have already put up. Afterward, you can warm yourselves with a hot chocolate from Le Pain Quotidien or a hot toddy from the bar at the Loeb Boathouse. *Pilgrim Hill is located at 72nd Street near Fifth Avenue, in Manhattan. Cedar Hill is located from 76th to 79th Streets near Fifth Avenue, in Manhattan. Subway: B, C to 72nd Street or 6 to 77th Street. Le Pain Quotidien is open seven days a week in the summer and Friday through Sunday in the winter. Hours vary depending on the season. Located inside the park at 69th Street, in Manhattan. 646-233-3768. www.lepainquotidien.com. Subway: 1 to 66 Street; B, C to 72 Street. The Loeb*

Gapstow Bridge in Central Park, with Fifth Avenue and 59th Street in the background

Boathouse is open seven days a week. Hours vary. Located inside the park near 75th Street and Fifth Avenue, in Manhattan. 212-517-2233. www.thecentralparkboathouse.com. Subway: 6 to 68th Street–Hunter College; B, C to 72nd Street; N, Q, R to Fifth Avenue–59th Street.

SPRING

Nothing captures the spark of new love like the first signs of spring in the city. The Conservatory Garden, a beautifully landscaped area in the northeastern corner of Central Park just above Museum Mile, is always one of the first places in town to burst into bloom, and consequently, it is a wonderful destination for a romantic stroll to appreciate the changing of the seasons. Even from the impressive wrought-iron gate that opens into the park from Fifth Avenue—the original entry gate to Cornelius Vanderbilt II's mansion, transplanted from its location fifty blocks farther south—the Conservatory Garden is a window onto a grand old New York of formal landscaping and classical European influences. Arranged into three equally striking horticultural vignettes, the garden in spring is a kaleidoscopic vision of bright colors amid the cold grays of Fifth Avenue and the muddy greens of the park. The manicured lawn of the central Italianate garden is lined with crabapple trees, which blossom in perfect rows of bright white and rich pink. The charming English garden unwinds in concentric circles of yellow and peach-colored flower beds from a lily pond in the center, where a sculptured fountain stands in tribute to Frances Hodgson Burnett's *The Secret Garden*. And the French garden, laid out in parterres of seasonal flowers, explodes in spring into a tapestry of tulips. Officially one of Central Park's quiet zones—and the most popular location in the park for weddings—the garden is a beautiful and peaceful place to celebrate the arrival of spring. *The Conservatory Garden is open seven days a week from 8:00 a.m. to dusk. Entrance at Fifth Avenue and East 105th Street, in Manhattan. www.centralparknyc.org/visit/things-to-see/north-end/conservatory-garden.html. Subway: 6 to 103rd Street.*

SUMMER

Few of the city's outdoor pleasures can compete with the special romance of an evening under the stars with the New York Philharmonic, which has serenaded an estimated 14 million people since these free outdoor concerts started in 1965. Every summer, the philharmonic plays a different program on two midsummer nights on the Great Lawn, in front of a diverse audience of dabblers and aficionados lounging on picnic blankets. (The concerts in Central Park are their signature events, but the New York Philharmonic also plays dates at one park in each of the other four boroughs.) The concerts begin at 8:00 p.m., but veterans and classical-music buffs start spreading their blankets before 6:00 p.m. The earlier you go, the closer you will be to the stage—but also the quieter you're expected to be. A more convivial atmosphere can be found farther out on the lawn, where people won't mind if you're munching on pâté while Brahms is being played. Per tradition, the concerts end with a round of fireworks, an idiosyncratic finishing touch on a one-of-a-kind New York evening. And if opera is more your style, the Metropolitan Opera also performs similar free recitals at Central Park's Summerstage each year. *New York Philharmonic concerts are usually held on two evenings in July, starting at 8:00 p.m., and are located on the Great Lawn, which is between West 79th and 85th Streets in the middle of the park, in Manhattan. For upcoming dates, call 212-875-5709 or visit www.nyphil.org. Subway: 4, 5, 6 to 86th Street; B, C to 81st Street–Museum of Natural History or 86th Street.*

AND WHEN EVENING COMES . . .

From majestic icons of luxury by the Park to charming inns hidden on less-traveled city streets, there are places to stay in New York to suit any romantic occasion. With a little planning and an eye for the part of town that suits you and your occasion best, you'll be able to find what you want—whether it's a seductive hideaway for a romantic break, the perfect hotel for your entire wedding party, or simply the most decadent honeymoon suite imaginable. Below are our suggestions for some of the most romantic hotels in New York.

CHELSEA PINES INN. A charming and friendly bed and breakfast in the heart of Chelsea. Rooms and common areas are decorated with classic film memorabilia (the owner's father ran movie theaters in Brooklyn) and there is a courtyard where guests can enjoy breakfast, or hold a small (up to ten person) wedding ceremony. **GOOD FOR**: Same-sex couples, those who want to stay somewhere with a real independent feel. *317 West 14th Street, between Eighth and Ninth Avenues, in Manhattan. www.chelseapinesinn.com. Subway: A, C, E, L to 14th Street-8th Avenue.*

CROSBY STREET HOTEL. Elegant inside and out, with beautiful suites and gardens on both sides of the building, the Crosby Street Hotel is remarkable for affording quiet romance in the heart of the sexy nightlife of SoHo and NoLIta. *79 Crosby Street between Prince and Spring Streets, in Manhattan. www.firmdalehotels.com/new-york/crosby-street-hotel. Subway: 6 to Spring Street; N, R to Prince Street.*

THE FOUR SEASONS. Classic luxury to the hilt. The rooms and suites are larger than many New York City apartments, many of which boast impeccable midtown and Central Park views, including one penthouse with a 360-degree panorama of the city. **GOOD FOR**: A landmark anniversary when money is no object. *57 East 57th Street between Park and Madison Avenues, in Manhattan. www.fourseasons.com/newyork. Subway: 4, 5 ,6, N, R, Q to 59th Street.*

THE JANE HOTEL. Darling of the West Village, the Jane is known as much for its old-fashioned bona fides (the original cabins–since chicly renovated—housed sailors and *Titanic* survivors in the early twentieth century) as for its star-studded guest list. Most of the rooms are famously small, but the Captain's Cabins feel elegant and indulgent, with views west over the Hudson. **GOOD FOR**: Younger couples on a budget who don't mind trading expansiveness for neighborhood. *113 Jane Street at West Street, in Manhattan. www.thejanenyc.com. Subway: A, C, E, L to 14th Street-8th Avenue.*

THE LAFAYETTE HOUSE. This little-known inn is housed in a NoHo brownstone, steps away from the chic shops and eateries of the Bowery. All rooms are individually decorated with antiques, and each has a working fireplace. Very private, very charming. **GOOD FOR**: Couples who want to be in the center of downtown, but have somewhere quiet to retire to. *38 East 4th Street, between Bowery and Lafayette Streets, in Manhattan. www.lafayettenyc.com. Subway: 6 to Bleecker Street.*

THE LIBRARY HOTEL. This centrally located "themed" hotel is infused with a love of literature. A block from the main branch of the New York Public Library, each floor is named for one of the categories in the Dewey Decimal system, and every guest room has a specially curated selection of books. The Love Suite has a private terrace and books personally chosen by Dr. Ruth Westheimer. **GOOD FOR**: Bibliophiles and those wanting romance in a convenient Manhattan location. *299 Madison Avenue at 41st Street, in Manhattan. www.libraryhotel.com. Subway: 4, 5, 6, 7, S to Grand Central; 7, B, D, F, M to 42nd Street-Bryant Park.*

THE MARITIME HOTEL. On the edges of Chelsea's gallery district, steps from the Highline, with views of the Hudson River Park, the Maritime is a charming hotel with nautical touches that only add to the sense of being stowed away in your own private place. Their bar and restaurant Bottega is one of the city's sexiest. **GOOD FOR**: Couples who want a taste of the nightlife. *363 West 16th Street at Ninth Avenue, in Manhattan. www.themaritimehotel.com. Subway: A, C, E, L to 14th Street-8th Avenue.*

THE MARK. This recently renovated Upper East Side stalwart is now a great mix of modern and luxury, with exquisite rooms and suites and impeccable-as-ever service. Jean-Georges Vongerichten's restaurant in the lobby is the perfect place for a romantic meal. **GOOD FOR**: Couples with a taste for the classics; those wanting a super luxurious experience. *25 East 77th Street between Madison and Fifth Avenues, in Manhattan. www.themarkhotel.com. Subway: 6 to 77th Street.*

MOUNT MORRIS HOUSE BED & BREAKFAST. A Harlem bed and breakfast in a landmarked residential area, housed in a thoughtfully restored Gilded-Age mansion. There are three suites (plus an apartment that sleeps six), featuring period details and fixtures such as fireplaces, plaster moldings, and beautiful wood floors. **GOOD FOR**: Architecture lovers, those looking for a love nest for a secret tryst. *12 Mount Morris Park West, between 121st and 122nd Streets, in Manhattan. www.mountmorrishousebandb.com. Subway: 2, 3 to 116th Street.*

STERLING HOUSE BED & BREAKFAST. This tiny, unlikely B&B has three quaint rooms, two in the main house and one private cottage. Owned by a husband and wife, Sterling House has all the trappings of a country B&B—lovely sitting rooms and gardens, delicious breakfasts—in the middle of Brooklyn. Though it's far from the big-name attractions in Manhattan, the subway is nearby, as is Prospect Park and the Brooklyn Botanic Garden. **GOOD FOR**: Couples who are familiar with New York and want something off the beaten path. *686 Sterling Place, between Franklin and Bedford Avenues, in Brooklyn. www.sterlingbedandbreakfast.com. Subway: 2, 3, 4, 5 or Shuttle to Franklin Avenue.*

Other romantic hotels featured in this book are the Carlyle (see pages 25, 163), the Gramercy Park Hotel (see page 43), the NoMad (see pages 67, 163), the Plaza (see page 163), the Waldorf Astoria (see page 163), and the Wythe (see pages 64, 163).

CHAPTER 2

GETTING TO KNOW
YOU BETTER

What happens after the first blush of romance has passed? When the tried-and-true methods of seduction have been tried and tried again? This is the moment for seeking out uncharted territory, for simpatico exploration, and for leaving the beaten paths. Fortunately for lovebirds, our city holds an untold number of nooks and crannies, and whether this is a first visit, a tenth visit, or the spot of your pied-à-terre, there are always treasures to discover when you look a bit beneath the surface. This chapter is about taking a little bit of a closer look at the charming details and subtle surprises in the city's most exciting, picturesque, and desirable neighborhoods.

In this chapter, we'll shine a spotlight, neighborhood by neighborhood, on some of the city's hidden gems and local fixtures, and sprinkle in a few lists of our favorite romantic attractions (fireplaces, gardens, and secret spaces) along the way. Rather than use these passages as specific itineraries, however, we encourage as much wandering as your schedule permits. The quieter parts of the city reveal themselves to you when you take it slow. Or, as the great sage Oscar Wilde once wrote, "the very essence of romance is uncertainty."

PLACES TO SEE AND BE SEEN

Everybody knows love and romance can find us at the least expected times and in the unlikeliest of places. But when you're seeking out the ideal setting for a lovely evening, trying to identify the right neighborhood for a romantic vacation, or even looking for the right place to set the mood for the big question, there are some parts of the city it's simply essential to explore first.

In choosing our favorite places to see and be seen, then, we are inevitably leaving out neighborhoods all over the five boroughs in favor of those parts of Manhattan and Brooklyn that are the best equipped to satiate appetites and fuel desires, and the most traveled by love-struck visitors to the city. Nowhere can rival Brooklyn Heights for the sheer beauty of its streets, or Long Island City for its views of the skyline; the boardwalks of Brighton Beach and Staten Island have a romance all their own; and people travel from all over the city to drop to one knee over dinner on Arthur Avenue in the Bronx. But those features alone might not be enough to define the full character of those neighborhoods. So take this section as an overview of those parts of the city already tailor-made for lovers. Stay here long enough, and you can discover the others for yourselves.

UNION SQUARE, FLATIRON, AND GRAMERCY

These three adjacent downtown *quartiers* are bound by three very different parks (Union Square on the south, Madison Square to the north, and Gramercy on the east) and brought together by a string of beautiful blocks, grand limestone skyscrapers, and Danny Meyer restaurants. **Union Square Park** *(14th to 17th Streets, between Broadway and Fourth Avenue)*—which sits atop the heart of lower Manhattan subway travel—is a bustling commons, home to the city's flagship farmers' market, as well as some shady lawns and a plaza that is one of the city's most pulsating public spaces. (If Robert Doisneau had taken *The Kiss* in New York, rather than in front of the Hôtel de Ville in Paris, he might have set it here.) The **farmers' market** *(www.grownyc.org/greenmarket/manhattan-union-square)* is open from 8:00 a.m. to 6:00 p.m. on Monday, Wednesday, Friday, and Saturday, filling the park's northern and western plazas with wares from farms, dairies, orchards, and vineyards all over the region. Though there are nearly seventy markets across the five boroughs, the Union Square market was one of the first (it started in 1976), and it is beloved by chefs, locals, and visitors from all over. (During peak season, the market sees more than 60,000 customers a day.) Saturdays in particular can be crowded, so instead, plan a trip in the early morning on one of the weekdays to explore the bounty of New York State and the surrounding areas: asparagus and snow peas in the spring; tomatoes, corn, stone fruit, and berries in the summer; apples, maple syrup, and root vegetables in the fall; and meat, eggs, jam, cheese, baked goods, and wines from the Finger Lakes and Long Island year-round. It is also a wonderful place to pick up a bouquet of wildflowers, the perfect peach, or a lovingly grown rose for your betrothed.

A block east, you'll arrive at Irving Place, a short, serene avenue named for the author Washington Irving, one of America's first men of letters. Irving never actually lived on the street, but he is nevertheless commemorated with a bust outside of Washington Irving High School, and a bronze plaque bearing his name is affixed to a townhouse on the corner of East 17th Street. (Two people that actually lived in this townhouse were decorator Elsie de Wolfe and her partner, the theater agent

Elisabeth Marbury. The couple referred to themselves as "the bachelors" and held weekly Sunday literary salons attended by turn-of-the-twentieth-century society scions and wits from the theater world.) The street is dotted with stately private homes (some have starred as luxurious lairs in such films as *Working Girl, The Devil's Own,* and *Arbitrage*) and extends south from **Gramercy Park** *(East 20th to 21st Streets, bounded by Park Avenue South and Third Avenue),* one of the city's two remaining gated parks, an impenetrable but beautifully maintained square that adds to the otherworldly charm of the area. A romantic walking tour of the area would not be complete without a stroll down East 19th Street between Third Avenue and Irving Place. This is called the Block Beautiful because of the mix of charming nineteenth- and early twentieth-century townhouses and urban cottages, some decorated with funky terra-cotta tile designs. (Look out for the tiny carriage house just off the southeast corner of Irving Place, with white trim, red doors, and a facade shaped like a wedding cake.) It's fun to imagine what the block was like in the early twentieth century, when neighbors and housemates George Bellows, Lillian Gish, Helen Hayes, and Ethel Barrymore invited friends F. Scott Fitzgerald and Eugene O'Neill over to pass an evening with champagne and lively partying. (Said Barrymore—from number 132—after leaving a soiree at the home of the novelist and critic Carl Van Vechten, who lived across the street at number 151: "I went there in the evening a young girl and came away in the morning an old woman.") Back on Irving Place, you'll find the sweet **Irving Farm Coffee Roasters** *(71 Irving Place, between East 18th and 19th Streets; www.irvingfarm.com)* tucked a few steps below street level. It has been in the neighborhood for nearly twenty years and borne witness to the boom of fancy coffee bars, the fetishizing of food, and the colonization of many of its brethren by Wi-Fi-enabled entrepreneurs. Irving Farm, however, does not boast either a fancy espresso machine or an Internet connection; instead, this is a convivial place to enjoy the simple treats of community and conversation, from early in the morning until the last glass and mug are bused. On a given day, you will likely spy at least one couple clearly on a first date, along with writers tapping on laptops, neighborhood fixtures enjoying the paper, and in the evening, young professionals stretching out with a glass of wine or a beer.

This area is one of the city's most important destinations for special occasion restaurants, a designation it owes in part to the presence of Danny Meyer. Known throughout the country and the world, Meyer's restaurants are perennially popular destinations for tourists and locals, and while he now has restaurants at MoMA, the Whitney, and in the Financial District, this is the neighborhood he began his now world-famous career in, when, in 1985, he opened the **Union Square Café** *(21 East 16th*

Street, between Union Square West and Fifth Avenue; www.unionsquarecafe.com), which cast a transformative glow across the formerly downtrodden area around the park. Nine years later, Meyer opened his second restaurant, **Gramercy Tavern** (*42 East 20th Street, between Park Avenue South and Broadway; www.gramercytavern.com*), which crystallized his signature hospitality-driven style of fine dining. At Gramercy Tavern, those with reservations enjoy their meals in a formal dining room adjacent to the walk-in-only tavern, and it's worth the wait for one of the first-come-first-served tavern dinner tables when you can sit at the bar with a cocktail and have the opportunity to drink in the vibrant New York atmosphere. **Maialino** is located in the **Gramercy Park Hotel** (*2 Lexington Avenue, between East 21st and 22nd Streets; www.maialinonyc.com*), which itself has shed its shabby look following an early-aughts renovation by hotelier Ian Schrager with the artist Julian Schnabel. (In its earlier heyday, the hotel was the site of Humphrey Bogart's first wedding and the intermittent residence of a mélange of twentieth-century notables, including the writers Edmund Wilson and Mary McCarthy and the family of Joseph P. Kennedy.) Maialino is Meyer's version of an Italian trattoria, and although it's on the ground floor, one of the restaurant's most alluring features is its view of Gramercy Park. Book a table for two for a springtime lunch, and when the sun shines through the lush treetops of Gramercy Park, you may feel as if New York is putting on a special show just for you. Meyer is also the man behind Shake Shack, the upscale burger joint now found in many cities and several different countries, whose original location is a shiny, futuristic structure at the foot of Madison Square Park.

This neighborhood is also a place to feast on architecture; in addition to the turn-of-the-century splendor around Gramercy Park, there is also the **Flatiron Building** (*175 Fifth Avenue between 22nd and 23rd Streets*), a triangular skyscraper from the early 1900s that looms over Broadway. The Flatiron is still in use as an office building, but you can gaze at its striking facade from the pedestrian plazas that surround it or from the inside of Madison Square Park. **The Metropolitan Life Tower** (*1 Madison Avenue at 23rd Street*), another landmark skyscraper, flanks the east side of Madison Square Park. *Subway: 4, 5, 6, L, N, Q, R to 14th Street–Union Square; 6 to 23rd Street; N, R to 23rd Street.*

NOLITA AND SOHO

As any veteran New Yorker will tell you, this part of the city is almost unrecognizable these days when compared to its former self. Now among the city's most expensive places to live and host to the greatest concentration of high-end stores and restaurants downtown, these adjoining neighborhoods epitomize the city's transition from the rough glamour of old New York to its more sophisticated incarnation today.

SoHo (which stands for South of Houston [Street]) inherited its architectural grandeur from its long industrial heritage and its cool from the shabby bohemia that would one day thrive in its lapsed factory buildings. NoLIta (an acronym for North of Little Italy) was once very much a part of the ethnic communities that are still concentrated in nearby Chinatown and Little Italy, before it absorbed the fashionable runoff of SoHo and the Lower East Side into its charming rows of brick townhouses.

Home to some of the city's best shopping—from chic major labels and department stores to unique boutiques and independents—the area is also one of the city's most beautiful, stretching from the stern iron-fronted buildings of SoHo's cobbled streets across to the smaller, quieter blocks and European-feeling café culture of NoLIta. While all of New York might be considered a walking town, these neighborhoods are particularly well suited to a leisurely stroll, with the most charming routes (and the most interesting places) to be found off the main drags of Broadway and Houston Street.

Whether you're in the mood for real shopping or simply the window variety, the few blocks between Lafayette Street to the east, Sixth Avenue to the west, Houston Street to the north, and Canal Street to the south are exceptionally pretty and inviting to walk around. The streets are cobbled and tree-lined, the buildings' facades are striking and eccentric, and the people watching is as much a distraction as the storefronts. And hidden away between the shops are some great places to pause for a quiet drink or a romantic meal. Across the street from an old church on Sullivan Street, on the western side of SoHo, is **The Room** (*144 Sullivan Street, between West Houston and Prince Streets*), a dark and cozy drinking spot with an exceptional range of wines and beers and a variety of comfortable candlelit corners in which to enjoy them. In the summer, the front windows open onto the street so the parade of SoHo's finest can provide the entertainment; in the cooler months, the Room feels as warm and intimate as a cabin in the woods. Heading east, the **Crosby Bar** at the Crosby Street Hotel (*79 Crosby Street, between Prince and Spring Streets; www.firmdalehotels.com/new-york/crosby-street-hotel/crosby-street-bar*) is a relatively new addition to the scene, and one that nicely balances the high and low tones that define the neighborhood. Accessible from Lafayette Street on one side or from the quieter Crosby Street on the other, the bar is large but seductively lit, and it somehow manages to feel like a secret in the heart of SoHo.

Lafayette Street itself is one of the most beautiful avenues downtown, bending and forking enough to distinguish itself from the grid and afford striking views of some of the extraordinary buildings that shade its sidewalks—from the old police headquarters down at 240 Centre Street to the magnificent Puck Building at Houston, whose part in New York legend began when the offices of *Puck Magazine* moved there in 1887, and was cemented when Billy Crystal's Harry finally declared his love for Meg Ryan's Sally in the ballroom there almost exactly a century later. The section of Lafayette between Prince and Broome Streets is particularly engaging and home to a number of the neighborhood's most romantic places to eat and drink. **Jack's Wife Freda** (*224 Lafayette Street, between Spring and Kenmare Streets; www.jackswifefreda.com*) is the sort of restaurant that keeps SoHo young at heart: small enough that patrons' elbows jostle for space, but lively enough—and with such wonderfully honest bistro-style food and wine—that by the end of dinner even the most besotted couple might feel as if they'd made a roomful of new friends. And farther down the street, the Swiss-inspired **Café Select** (*212 Lafayette Street, between Spring and Kenmare Streets; www.cafeselectnyc.com*) has quickly become the hub of the sort of town square that has grown up around the intersections of Lafayette, Spring, and Kenmare Streets. Tables at the windows offer a picturesque view of the redesigned park on Cleveland Place (itself a great place to sit among hipsters and tourists and people watch), the buzzing crowds that gather around the enduringly hip restaurant (and secret subterranean bar) **La Esquina** (*114 Kenmare Street, between Lafayette and Centre Streets; www.esquinanyc. com*), and the row of townhouses reminiscent of old New York across the way.

Down on Spring Street, avoid the touristy crowds that gather outside Lombardi's pizzeria, with its invitations to waiting parties booming out over the P.A., and instead seek out a pastry or two at **Ceci Cela** (*55 Spring Street between Mulberry and Lafayette Streets; www.cecicelanyc.com*), a local institution and one of the sweetest bakeries in the city. Ceci Cela provides croissants and other indulgent treats for several restaurants and delicatessens around town—even as far as Brooklyn and Queens—and you can buy their legendary all-butter croissants frozen by the dozen for home consumption. But nothing beats picking one up fresh from the oven in the store and taking it with a cup of coffee or a freshly squeezed orange juice to the park at the corner of Spring and Mulberry Streets, where you can pause on a quiet bench beneath a tree and plan out the rest of your day in style.

Head east from Lafayette along Prince Street into the heart of NoLIta, where street markets open up on weekends along the crumbling brick walls of St. Patrick's Old Cathedral, and where the larger brands and famous restaurants of SoHo give way to smaller shops and trendier haunts. One of the best-stocked and most attractive bookstores in the city, **McNally Jackson** (*52 Prince Street, between Lafayette and Mulberry Streets; www.mcnallyjackson.com*) draws the sexiest downtown literati to a

great calendar of events, from readings by authors both local and iconic to talks in the annual New Yorker Festival. Alongside books and a well-curated collection of magazines, it has a charming café that's always busy without being noisy, filled with a pleasant crowd of visiting people watchers and studious locals. So pick a book, order a coffee, and wait for someone to flirtatiously challenge your apparent interest in the nineteenth-century Russian gothic (or whatever else happens to be the volume at hand). And a block farther east, at Mott Street, **Cafe Gitane** (*242 Mott Street, between East Houston and Prince Streets; www.cafegitanenyc.com*) boasts the most hotly contested tables in all of NoLIta, precisely because they offer the prettiest views of the prettiest people—and the churchyard of the cathedral opposite. Sitting over a coffee or a pressed lemonade at Gitane (which also has an outpost in the Jane Hotel in the West Village) is something of a local spectator sport: while you watch your fellow customers and passersby, you'll be observed by the strolling throngs outside—and if you're lucky, on a weekend you might get to watch a wedding party go by, too. *Subway: 6 to Spring Street; B, D, F, M to Broadway–Lafayette Street; N, R to Prince Street.*

EAST VILLAGE AND LOWER EAST SIDE

Downtown on the east side does not, admittedly, offer some of the obvious trappings of romance and beauty. Charm here is often characterized by a measure of grit and awkwardness, as many of the best restaurants and bars are wedged into tiny, dim spaces, with few tables and no-reservation policies. But it's also an area where it's easy to find intimacy over candlelight, across a simple two-top, or huddled on barstools. And stuffed into these tiny storefronts are heaps of talented artists, chefs, mixologists, designers, and small-business owners, whose striving to do their own thing in the center of Manhattan adds an urgency and authenticity to the experience.

Unlike the West Village, the Upper East Side, and Upper West Side, the East Village and the Lower East Side were not built for the rich. Though rents here today are among the priciest in the city, this area's heritage is as an immigrant neighborhood, and later, a crucible of music, poetry, and art, and this legacy is imprinted on the streets in pretty and not-so-pretty ways. The architecture here (though dotted, as in so many neighborhoods, with new development) is not dominated by townhouses and limestone facades, but rather by the humble faces of tenement buildings. On the other hand, the flavors of the melting pot the neighborhood once was are still palpable (on Sundays, you can find church services in Polish, Ukrainian, Italian, and Chinese all within a few blocks of one another) and give the place a whiff of the popular adage that if you can make it here, you can make it anywhere. This is especially true when it comes to dining. This is the birthplace of David Chang's Momofuku empire and Gabrielle Hamilton's famous boîte, **Prune** (*54 East 1st Street, between First and Second Avenues; www.prunerestaurant.com*). But long before this new wave of talent arrived, the area was a destination for a mind-boggling number of different international specialties. The East Village is still where you can find some of the city's best ramen, pierogi, and cannoli. The Lower East Side is widely known as having been the center of Jewish immigration in the city, but it's also essentially the crossroads of Little Italy and Chinatown. **Katz's Delicatessen** (*205 East Houston Street, between Orchard and Ludlow Streets; www.katzsdelicatessen.com*), the site of the famous orgasm scene in *When Harry Met Sally*, still does a brisk business, as does the 120-year-old Italian bakery **Veniero's** (*342 East 11th Street, between First and Second Avenues; www.venierospastry. com*) and **Veselka** (*144 Second Avenue at 9th Street; www.veselka.com*), a twenty-four-hour Ukrainian diner on Second Avenue that's been fueling the neighborhood's underemployed coffeehouse bards for sixty years. If you can save your appetite and want to look beyond these stalwarts, you'll be rewarded with some more intimate gems: the rustic, crimson-colored pasta nook **Porsena** (*21 East 7th Street, between Third and Second Avenues; www.porsena.com*); the brothers Grimm–inspired **Edi & the Wolf** (*102 Avenue C, between East 6th and 7th Streets; www.ediandthewolf.com*) for wonderful Austrian food; and **Northern Spy Food Co.** (*511 East 12th Street between Avenues A and B; www.northernspyfoodco.com*), which serves what might be called American, close-to-the-land cuisine—to name just a few of the many, many worthy dining spots here.

These neighborhoods are also home to serious cocktail culture. The influence of secretive cocktail-driven spots Milk & Honey (which has left the neighborhood for less discreet digs in east midtown and **PDT** (still standing—albeit invisibly—behind the phone booth of a hot-dog joint; see page 73) can be seen in the new generation of mixologist-proprietors that have opened shop all over the area—this is the neighborhood to woo someone over an exceptional Manhattan. **The Summit Bar** (*133 Avenue C, between East 8th and 9th Streets; www.thesummitbar.net*), **Pouring Ribbons** (*225 Avenue B, between East 13th and 14th Streets, second floor; www.pouringribbons.com*), and **Booker and Dax**, which doubles as the antechamber to **Momofuku Ssäm Bar** (*207 Second Avenue, between East 12th and 13th Streets; www.momofuku.com/new-york/booker-and-dax/*) are a few that stand out—but as with the restaurants, new spots are always popping up, and part of the appeal of this neighborhood is that it's so easy to stumble into somewhere unassuming and truly great.

Aside from eating and drinking, another beautiful draw to the area are the large numbers of community gardens. There are thirty-nine in between 14th Street and

Houston alone—one for just about every block. Many of these gardens date from the 1970s, when, in an effort to prevent vacant lots from being colonized by drug users, neighbors turned those lots into gardens. Most of the surviving gardens are still maintained by community members, and every garden has its own board and legislature. They are all beautiful, intimate nooks to stumble upon and wander through, or to sit and pass the time in quiet company. But perhaps they feel the most special for all the things they are not: they are not crowded; they are not overrun; and they are definitely not what one would expect to find tucked between row houses and small condos.

If there's one idea that sums up this vibrant neighborhood, it's the interplay between history and change. Whether it's the influence of the early strivers, who left an indelible mark on the neighborhood during their bids for better lives in this city, or its legacy as the place that the Beat Poets, Allen Ginsberg, '80s artists, and punk rockers claimed to seek out their counterculture, or just a self-perpetuating loop of the history of cool laying the groundwork for more cool to be produced, this neighborhood has long been a place where you feel past, present, and future all together. *Subway: 6 to Astor Place; L to First Avenue; F to Second Avenue; B, D to Grand Street; F, J, M to Delancey–Essex Streets.*

CHELSEA AND THE MEATPACKING DISTRICT

In New York, a few blocks—or a few years—can make all the difference. Just across town from the East Village, and sandwiched between the West Village, the Flatiron, and the southern side of midtown Manhattan, Chelsea and the Meatpacking District are two of the city's most distinctive and most dramatically transformed areas. These adjacent neighborhoods, which cover a stretch of the west side that runs roughly from West 14th Street through the West 20s, and from Eighth Avenue all the way west to the Hudson River, have their roots in industry and labor—but they occupy an altogether more indulgent place in New York City life today.

The Meatpacking District—originally known as Gansevoort Market—was once, as its name suggests, Manhattan's most vital and active market for wholesale butchers, a place that lay dormant during the day but came alive in the small hours of the night, and seemed as mysterious and exciting to a visitor as it was indispensable to the city's restaurateurs and delicatessens. In the latter half of the twentieth century, other facets of nocturnal New York life sprang up alongside the market, and the area became one of the city's edgier nightspots, with bars, clubs, and twenty-four-hour restaurants catering to increasingly eclectic downtown crowds. (It was also a fitting backdrop to Michael Douglas's fatal attraction to Glenn Close. . . .) While the butchers and the edgy spots have since moved elsewhere—priced out of the neighborhood by an influx of fancy restaurants, bars, nightclubs, and exclusive hotels—the Meatpacking District still comes alive at night, albeit more with the sounds of cabs and high heels on cobblestones than the calls of butchers and the noises of trucks.

And a few blocks north, the cobblestones turn back to concrete in Chelsea, one of Manhattan's most beautiful residential neighborhoods, with a historic brownstone district encompassing several blocks of pretty townhouses and some of the city's finest art deco apartment buildings. It, too, still bears the marks of its industrial heritage, in its wide streets, its architecture, and its access to the piers at the Hudson. These days, Chelsea is famed for being one of the art centers of the world, home to dozens of the most influential galleries and collections of all kinds and periods of art—with many of the neighborhood's large old factory buildings and warehouses having been converted into immaculate exhibition spaces. It's also known as one of the historically gay meccas of New York, with many of the city's most popular gay bars and clubs lining Eighth and Ninth Avenues.

One thing that connects these neighborhoods—literally, and in spirit—is the **High Line** (*Gansevoort to West 30th Streets, roughly above Tenth Avenue; www.thehighline. org*). The elevated park on the west side is many things—a sophisticated example of forward-thinking urban planning, an ingenious redressing of the city's industrial skeleton, and a beautifully landscaped park, to name a few. But more than the rest, it is somewhere to walk and people watch, to look and be looked at—the ultimate gallery in a part of town famous for them. The Diller–von Furstenberg Sundeck, just north of West 14th Street at Tenth Avenue, is the most glamorous of the park's resting spots, lined with wooden lounge chairs that can be rolled into your preferred position (perhaps alongside another?) on the old railroad tracks embedded in the pathway—the ideal spot from which to coolly observe passersby. And the carefully manicured lawns between West 22nd and 23rd Streets, flanked with comfortable wooden bleachers and carts for snacks and drinks, are ideal for the bolder among us to stretch out in the sun on warmer days and watch the world go by—so long as you don't mind being watched yourself by the neighbors in the buildings nearby. The High Line extends from Gansevoort Street through the heart of the Meatpacking District and by 2015 is due to reach up through all of Chelsea to West 34th Street, where the old tracks come to a peaceful end in former railway yards overlooking the Hudson.

At the southern end of the High Line, a relatively new addition to the Meatpacking District is the **Standard Hotel** (*848 Washington Street, between West 13th and Little West 12th Streets; www.standardhotels.com/high-line*). Famed for its floor-to-ceiling

glass windows, which have been known to present guests with the opportunity to explore their exhibitionistic sides, the Standard has also given the neighborhood some of its sexier new distractions, from the ice rink it opens in the winter months (*see page 28*) to Le Bain, its bar and club in the penthouse on the roof, which is one of the more fabulous (if overly popular) places for a late-night drink downtown. Until the arrival of the Standard, the **Gansevoort** (*18 Ninth Avenue, between West 13th and Little West 12th Streets; www.hotelgansevoort.com*) was the best-known hotel in the Meatpacking District, with one of the fanciest rooftop bars in town. From up here, you can look down on **Soho House**'s (*29–35 Ninth Avenue, between West 13th and 14th Streets; www.sohohouseny.com*) modest rooftop pool, gaze out across the Hudson to the lights of Jersey City, or just bask in the twinkle of the city's glow—and because

The public amphitheater on the High Line in Chelsea, which has a view over Tenth Avenue the bar has several terraces facing out in different directions, it's often the case that you can choose between joining the lively crowds on one side or finding a secluded spot with a pretty view on the other. If a quiet, romantic meal is what you're looking for, the charming **Paradou** *(8 Little West 12th Street, between Washington Street and Ninth Avenue; www.paradounyc.com)* is one of the neighborhood's more understated nooks, reliably free of the all-night revelers that frequent the bars, terraces, and dance clubs that line the Meatpacking's cobblestone alleys. The restaurant's cozy front room leads to a large, enclosed garden room in the back, which is covered and heated for year-round use, the perfect complement to Paradou's Provence cuisine, including a special foie gras tasting menu.

Walk north on the High Line, over the cobbled and boutique-lined streets of the Meatpacking District, and descend at West 23rd Street into the heart of Chelsea's gallery district. Whether you're exploring idly on a weekend, mingling with the unique crowd of art lovers and pseuds, or joining the chic and celebratory throngs who line the blocks of galleries on opening nights during the week, the area has a style that translates into a peculiar New York romance. Alongside the art itself, two of the city's best and most interesting bookshops sit across from one another on Tenth Avenue. **Printed Matter** *(195 Tenth Avenue, between West 21st and 22nd Streets; www.printedmatter.org)* is an independent bookstore in the truest sense, stocking (and in some cases publishing) a staggering range of artists' books, pamphlets, magazines, and monographs—most of which you won't find anywhere else in the city. And **192 Books** *(192 Tenth Avenue, between West 21st and 22nd Streets; www.192books.com)*, while more conventional, relatively speaking, is one of the best curated independent shops around, with a program of intimate readings and talks that bring a discriminating audience into its tiny but charming space. In between gallery stops—or after you're through with walking around for the day—there are some wonderful places for anything from a quiet drink to a romantic dinner. **Le Grainne Cafe** *(183 Ninth Avenue, between West 21st and 22nd Streets; www.legrainnecafe. com)* is one of the most authentically French bistros in Manhattan: small and perpetually busy, but cozy and informal enough to set everybody at ease, it's the perfect place for a crepe and a *citron pressé* in the middle of a lazy afternoon. **Cookshop** *(156 Tenth Avenue, between West 19th and 20th Streets; www.cookshopny.com)*, owned by the trio of chefs and entrepreneurs who run NoHo's successful Five Points brasserie, is a more energetic and flashy spot for a dinner date, with a bustling yet sophisticated feel that is just right for the post-gallery (or pre-nightclub) crowd. And **Bottino** *(246 Tenth Avenue, between West 24th and 25th Streets; www.bottinonyc.com)* is something of a traditional spot for late-night dinners after an opening at a gallery, with a colorful clientele that comes for the fine Italian food and wine and stays for the rather secretive garden. *Subway: C, E at 23rd Street; A, C, E at 14th Street; L at Eighth Avenue.*

WEST VILLAGE

Oh, beautiful West Village, home to Manhattan's most charming streets. It's so easy to feel romantic while wandering Jane, Barrow, Bedford, and Grove, getting lost in these brownstone-lined streets with nary a skyscraper in sight. The West Village can roughly be defined as west of Sixth Avenue, between West 14th and Houston Streets, with the heart of the village found in the winding, numberless streets between Jane and Leroy. The quaint area is enveloped by a collection of ever more upscale boutiques on Bleecker (the West Village's answer to Madison Avenue), and Hudson Streets, the latter of which is actually an avenue populated with bars, restaurants, grocery stores, Laundromats, and other reminders of big-city life. When you've walked as far west as you can go, you'll hit Hudson River Park, framed by two verdant piers that extend over the water from Charles and Christopher Streets, respectively, which are both lovely places for a leisurely picnic and a nap on a summer day.

There really is no better neighborhood than the West Village for a hand-in-hand walk, and as you wander the crisscrossing streets, look out for 75½ Bedford, the city's narrowest townhouse, and its neighbor, 77 Bedford, the oldest house in the Village, which was built in 1799. The townhouse at 75½ Bedford has been the residence of poet Edna St. Vincent Millay, the actor John Barrymore, the anthropologist Margaret Mead, and Cary Grant (who is rumored to have lived here with a boyfriend early in his acting career). Another street to hit is the diminutive Minetta Lane, a quirky two-block alley with a rocky past. The street began its life as a creek in the 1600s; later it achieved land-based notoriety as a destination for emancipated slaves known as Little Africa. In the late nineteenth century, owing to some rough bars in the neighborhood, it was declared one of "the most enthusiastically murderous thoroughfares in the city" by the *New York Herald*, and then it finally came full circle in 1973, when number 5–7 Minetta Lane was chosen as the home of Al Pacino's whistle-blowing cop in *Serpico*. On the corner of Minetta and MacDougal Street stands **Cafe Wha?** (*115 MacDougal Street, between Minetta Lane and West 3rd Street; www.cafewha.com*), where Bob Dylan played his first gig in New York; he actually played at the original location next door, but the reincarnation milks the rock legend for all it's worth. A more romantic rest stop in the area is the **Mermaid Oyster Bar** (*79 MacDougal Street, between Bleecker and West Houston Streets; www.themermaidnyc.com/oyster/*), which is full

of little tables for two and has the most civilized happy hour in the neighborhood: $1 oysters and $7 maritime-themed cocktails. And across Sixth Avenue a few blocks north from Minetta Lane is the lovely coffee shop **Joe** (*141 Waverly Place, between Gay Street and Sixth Avenue; www.joenewyork.com*), a community fixture that offers superior espresso drinks and hosts an all-day mingling of locals, writers, and coffeehouse dreamers. Get there early on a weekend morning to claim a table and witness the ebb and flow of a cross section of beautiful Villagers, or lace up your shoes to join their informal running club on Saturday morning. The group welcomes visitors and novices—runners get a free beverage of their choice, and in addition to clocking thousands of miles, the group has also logged several lasting couplings.

New York is a city that rewards wanderers, and the West Village is a treasure chest for ambling pedestrians, packed with alluring cocktail spots, glittering shop

A West Village street

windows, and endlessly charming cafés and restaurants, and part of the fun is seeing what gem you stumble across. But if you want to plan in advance for a special meal, try making a reservation at **Wallsé** (*344 West 11th Street, between Washington and Greenwich Streets; www.kg-ny.com/wallse*), an airy, elegant restaurant that serves Austrian cuisine in a small, white-walled, contemporary art–filled dining room one block from the river. And although every upscale brand worth knowing about has a West Village storefront these days, if you can find your way through the gridless maze to **Three Lives & Company** (*154 West 10th Street, between Waverly Place and Seventh Avenue South; www.threelives.com*), you can reward yourself with a book from every West Villager's favorite bookstore.

What the West Village is not home to are any museums, big parks, or showy landmarks; instead, a pair of lovebirds can easily pass an afternoon meandering from corner to beautiful corner, dreaming about which of the perfect historic townhouses they'd buy if money were no object. *Subway: A, B, C, D, E, F, M to West 4th Street–Washington Square; 1 to Christopher Street–Sheridan Square.*

MIDTOWN

To a tourist or newcomer to the city, midtown can seem at first like little more than a labyrinth of concrete and glass filled with the footsteps of a million bustling business makers. But, as you'd expect from the heart of one of the biggest business centers in the world, there are places of respite and havens of nourishment, calm, and even romance among the skyscrapers—indoor gardens, hidden parks, bars, restaurants, and cafés that can transport you from the stress of the street to a better place.

Framed by the grand public library and the giant towers of 42nd Street, **Bryant Park** (*Between West 40th and 42nd Streets and Fifth and Sixth Avenues*) is an oasis in midtown and one of the most beautiful parks in the city. Between the cafés nearby, the majesty of the library and the surrounding buildings, and the events that occupy the lawn—from an ice rink in winter to the series of evening movies in the summer (*see page 30*)—it's also a great place to sit, observe, and be observed by an eclectic and smart crowd. Go in the afternoon and get a snack from the 'wichcraft kiosk, or go at night and sip a drink on the balcony of the Bryant Park Grill.

Head east along the grand passage of 42nd Street, and on the easternmost side of midtown lies another of the city's great underappreciated oases: **Tudor City** (*Between East 40th and 43rd Streets and First and Second Avenues*). Featuring the first residential skyscraper in the world, and a historic landmark, the Tudor City complex is a relic of New York's glorious heyday. Standing in front of the towers of apartments—which are still some of the most sought-after places in midtown—is one of the two original gardens designed to serve the complex when it was built in the 1920s. Little known to visitors, ignored by harried working midtown denizens, and underused by busy residents, the garden, open to the public, is a surreal and beautiful setting for a walk, a picnic, or just a cup of coffee and a conversation.

Not far from the parks, one of the oldest hotels in midtown still maintains one of the city's most beautiful and lively bars. Celebrated first for hosting Dorothy Parker and her literary chums at the legendary Round Table, and later for accommodating a cat whose prowling presence became synonymous with the eccentric glamour of the place, the **Algonquin Hotel** (*59 West 44th Street, between Fifth and Sixth Avenues; www.algonquinhotel.com*) is a relic of the booming Manhattan of the early twentieth century, with a bar and lounge that manages to be both cavernous and intimate, lavishly decorated in colonial style with vast armchairs and wood paneling. Secure yourself a cozy table for two around the outskirts of the room, and you can pass a good hour or two of intimate conversation and uninterrupted people watching over excellent old-fashioned cocktails.

While shopping in midtown is an undeniable draw—and one of the defining features of the area—it's also one of the busiest and most exhausting activities the city has to offer. But during the holiday season, walking up Fifth Avenue from the 40s to Central Park is a treat. As well as the occasional street decoration—stars and snowflakes of lights that hang delicately above the traffic—the avenue is lit up by some of the most inventive and extravagant decorations ever to grace a storefront. Icons of Manhattan consumerism, from Tiffany & Co. to Bergdorf Goodman, Barneys, Cartier, and Hermès, cover their buildings in giant ribbons and jewelry, shroud their windows under elaborate wreaths of glass and lights, and orchestrate window displays that fall somewhere between a haute runway show and an opera.

And if all that shopping (or window-shopping) wears you out, seek one of midtown's superlative rooftops. Take the tiny, wood-paneled, old-fashioned elevator from the lobby to the penthouse at the **Peninsula Hotel** (*700 Fifth Avenue, between East 54th and 55th Streets; newyork.peninsula.com*), order a drink or two, and choose whether you want to look out over the city or up Fifth Avenue to Central Park. On a clear night, you can see the lights of Harlem on the horizon and their reflections dancing in the reservoir in the Park. Or for something more intimate, sneak behind the New York Public Library at Bryant Park and find the **Bookmarks** bar (*299 Madison Avenue, between East 41st and 42nd Streets; www.hospitalityholdings.com*), on the roof of the Library Hotel (*see page 36*). Though much smaller than the Peninsula's, the

Bookmarks terrace is charming, with views over midtown and into Bryant Park, and it has the quality of making you feel you've traveled through time to an older, more civilized New York. *Subway: 4, 5, 6 to Grand Central–42nd Street; 7 to Grand Central–42nd Street or Fifth Avenue; B, D, F, M to 42nd Street–Bryant Park.*

UPPER EAST SIDE

The Upper East Side is the capital of swank, the birthplace of the phrase "ladies who lunch," and a bastion of good taste. The locals who stroll Park, Madison, and Fifth Avenues are typically well-groomed, buttoned-up, and impeccably turned out. Chanel purses, Goyard totes, and Ralph Lauren blazers make frequent appearances on the sidewalk, and even the little children are a sight to behold, in their pleated prep-school jumpers and mini blazers with embroidered crests. Skip the eastern avenues, which are filled with frat-boy bars and new high-rises, and instead turn your gaze on all that lies west of Lexington Avenue. Park Avenue boasts the grandest residential buildings; Madison, the upscale shopping area; and Fifth is where you will find the Met *(see page 17)*, the Frick *(see page 59)*, the Guggenheim *(1071 Fifth Avenue, between East 88th and 89th Streets; www.guggenheim.org)*, and the other institutions of Museum Mile. If you need a respite from the bigness of the city, try wandering above East 86th Street to a small neighborhood known as Carnegie Hill. This area, one of the most exclusive residential areas in the city, is named for steel magnate Andrew Carnegie, whose mansion on East 91st Street and Fifth Avenue is now home to the **Cooper-Hewitt, National Design Museum** *(2 East 91st Street, between Fifth and Madison Avenues; www.cooperhewitt.org)*. Here, you can treat your betrothed to the civilized charms of a brunch at **Sarabeth's** *(see page 93)*, an afternoon in the design museum, and possibly a glimpse of New York's love-story laureate, Woody Allen, who lives nearby. Up here you will also find a few special one-off shops, such as **Blue Tree** *(1283 Madison Avenue, between East 91st and 92nd Streets; www.bluetreenyc.com)*, the Upper East Side's answer to a quirky curiosity shop (and a great place to pick up a cool, unusual piece of jewelry), and the **Corner Bookstore** *(1313 Madison Avenue, between East 92nd and 93rd Streets; www.cornerbookstorenyc.com)*, a nearly forty-year-old, one-room bookshop that's magically filled with every book you need (and plenty that you won't be able to live without).

Central Park is the obvious choice for local greenery, but the lesser-traveled **Carl Schurz Park** *(East End Avenue between East 84th and 90th Streets)* is a more intimate and equally romantic spot. Named for a nineteenth-century German-born statesman, the park was derelict until the 1970s, when a neighborhood group took on its refurbishment. Today, it is bursting with lush gardens and graceful staircases, and it boasts a close-up look at Gracie Mansion (the official residence of New York City's mayor), as well as views across the East River and Wards Island. (If you'd actually like to get inside the mansion, try visiting on a Wednesday, when tours are offered.) Likewise, the **Met** (*see page 17*) is the museum everyone thinks of in these parts, but there are plenty of other gems around (they don't call this Museum Mile for nothing), many of them housed in buildings as grand as the art they hold inside. The

The façade of the Frick Collection, on the Upper East Side

suggestive work of Egon Schiele and Gustav Klimt is displayed in the beautiful **Neue Galerie** (*1048 Fifth Avenue, between East 85th and 86th Streets; www.neuegalerie.org*), alongside a tremendous collection of early-twentieth-century paintings and decorative art from Germany and Austria. The **Museum of the City of the New York** (*1220 Fifth Avenue, between East 103rd and 104th Streets; www.mcny.org*) is an interesting museum that showcases art, history, and culture related to the city. And then there is the **Frick Museum** (*1 East 70th Street, between Fifth and Madison Avenues; www.frick.org*), the unequivocally grand museum-mansion on Fifth Avenue and East 70th Street. Housed in the home of steel magnate Henry Clay Frick, the museum has paintings, drawings, sculpture, furniture, and metalworks from the Renaissance through the nineteenth century. It is surrounded by gardens and separated from the street by an iron gate, which reminds visitors of its earlier incarnation as an expansive private home right in the middle of Manhattan. In the spring, three grand old magnolia trees grace the avenue with their pink floral bursts. But perhaps even more special than the outdoor greenery is the Garden Court, an indoor conservatory with a beautiful arched glass ceiling and Ionic stone columns. The benches there are a lovely place to relax between exhibitions, but the lush, elegant setting could also double as a proposal spot. *Subway: 4, 5, 6 to 86th Street; 6 to 77th, 96th, or 103rd Streets.*

UPPER WEST SIDE

Reaching from Columbus Circle and the northern edge of the Theater District all the way up the Hudson side of Manhattan to Harlem, the Upper West Side is in many ways the classic face of Manhattan. Like its eastern counterpart across the park, the west side is steeped in history and is a happy mixture of residential neighborhoods and old New York institutions. But where the east has Museum Mile, Park Avenue, and all the glamour of Fifth and Madison Avenues, the landscape of the west side is quieter and more austere, and its landmarks are less beacons of culture and commerce than monuments to New York's own glorious past.

Everybody knows that Central Park is *the* park, and **Central Park West** is arguably its most beautiful and hallowed side. It's along here that crowds gather to watch the Macy's Thanksgiving Day Parade, and it's in the lots in the back of the American Museum of Natural History where smart parents bring their kids to catch a surreal glimpse of the giant balloons being inflated the night before. Some of the city's most famous apartment buildings are here, including the Dakota, home for many years to such luminaries as John Lennon, Lauren Bacall, Rudolf Nureyev, and Jerry Seinfeld. And with only the American Museum of Natural History at its curb, this side of the park is perennially quieter than the east side and almost always a more pleasant place for a walk.

But across the Upper West Side is another of New York's great treasures: **Riverside Park**. Stretching up the western edge of Manhattan, roughly from West 63rd Street to West 129th Street in Harlem, Riverside Park defines the grandest quarter of Manhattan's borders and, even as close as it is to the Henry Hudson Parkway and the buzz of traffic up the west side, is one of the most pleasant parks for walking or picnicking. Like much of the architecture of the Upper West Side, the park bears the influences of nineteenth-century tastes and fashions, and as a result it has a European feel to it. Walk north on a nice afternoon and you'll come across the Hamilton Fountain, for example, at West 76th Street and Riverside Drive—a beautiful carving set into the stone wall that used to be a drinking spot for horses on their way uptown more than a century ago. Farther up, just north of the charming crabapple grove at West 91st Street, the Joan of Arc memorial stands proudly in front of the imposing residential buildings across the street and makes this part of the walkway beside the park feel more like the embankment of the Seine than the Hudson. But the most beautiful stretch of the park is its last twenty blocks or so, across the river from the Palisades, where the pathway becomes Cherry Walk—a carefully manicured avenue lined with cherry trees, which winds north alongside the Hudson and culminates in Sakura Park, a decorative garden landscaped a century ago with cherry trees donated by the Japanese government as a gift to the city. The trees still bloom in unison every spring, and they transform this part of the city into a paradise of soft whites and pinks, making it the perfect environment for a romantic evening in spring or summer.

The old-fashioned and European feel of this part of the city extends beyond the architecture and the landscape to the food and culture within. While the Upper West Side doesn't share the sheer volume or high turnover of chic new restaurants that you find downtown, on the Upper East Side, or in trendier parts of Brooklyn, it instead has a disproportionate number of the classics. Jean-Georges Vongerichten's eponymous flagship restaurant (*1 Central Park West, between West 60th and 61st Streets; www.jean-georgesrestaurant.com*) boasts one of the most seductive dining rooms in the city, with stunning views out of its large colonial windows into the park and an equally beautiful menu. At **Ouest** (*2315 Broadway, between West 83rd and 84th Streets; www.ouestny.com*), over on Broadway, the food is still high-end French cuisine, but the atmosphere is more suited to bustling banquettes than immaculate tablecloths. And the long-standing locals' favorite **Cafe Luxembourg** (*200 West 70th Street, between*

West End and Amsterdam Avenues; www.cafeluxembourg.com) sits somewhere between the two, an elegant and romantic restaurant that won't feel too stuffy—ideal for a surprise proposal, rather than a more obvious one.

For many lifelong New Yorkers and visitors to the Upper West Side, all that is good about this part of town emanates from **Lincoln Center** *(10 Lincoln Center Plaza, between West 62nd and 65th Streets; www.lincolncenter.org)*, the large complex of buildings and venues in the mid-60s between Columbus and Amsterdam Avenues. The heart of the city's cultural establishment and an institution on par with the Barbican or the Louvre, Lincoln Center is home to some of New York's finest arts and entertainment. From the Metropolitan Opera to the New York City Ballet, and from adventurous new theater to the New York Film Festival, Lincoln Center hosts a program of incredible events year-round to suit all manner of tastes. With its main complex built up around the beautiful Josie Robertson Plaza *(see page 23)* and a modernist landscape of fountains, balconies, terraces, and impressive flights of steps, it's also a wonderful place to people watch and the backdrop for countless romantic nights out. This is one of the few places in the city where you can expect on any given night to find tuxedos and cocktail dresses alongside sneakers and skinny jeans—dates to Lincoln Center can range from a cappuccino at the café in Alice Tully Hall before an art-house movie to a champagne supper during the intermission of an opera. And given the grandeur and history of the surroundings, it can be just as romantic either way. *Subway: 1, A, B, C, D to 59th Street–Columbus Circle or 125th Street; 1 to 66th Street–Lincoln Center.*

WILLIAMSBURG

If we had written this book ten years ago, it might have been a stretch to suggest that Williamsburg, a large swath of the western edge of Brooklyn that peeks at lower Manhattan from across the East River, was endearing enough to merit a special trip across the water. It is—and we might as well get this out of the way—not the city's prettiest neighborhood, by picture-postcard standards. But thanks to the clustering of boutique hotels and Michelin-starred chefs, Williamsburg has come out of an awkward period of adolescence and developed into an idiosyncratically attractive, if still a little raw, destination. It has also sprouted appealing features like a waterfront park and some of the most delicious food and drink in the city.

The history of Williamsburg echoes the thematic ebb and flow seen all over New York, and as in so much of the city, the neighborhood's modern gentrification has been met with tension between commercial and aesthetic improvements and the marginalization, displacement, and homogenization that this development has caused. The neighborhood was born in the early 1800s, when what had been the thoroughfare for goods grown on the Bushwick farmland was developed into a getaway for Manhattanites and christened Williamsburg for the surveyor, Jonathan Williams. Eventually, the area swelled, its bucolic character gave way to industry, and Williamsburg became a source of production for several important nineteenth- and twentieth-century industries: shipbuilding, sugar, and brewing. (In 1849, Pfizer Pharmaceuticals was founded in the Broadway Triangle area of South Williamsburg.) Ornate structures of commerce like the domed banking palace at 175 Broadway (a glorious National Historic Landmark whose opulent interior was recently restored, and which is now an events space and banquet hall) reflected the area's ascent, and at one point during the nineteenth century, Williamsburg contained 10 percent of the country's wealth. In the 1900s, the completion of the Williamsburg Bridge initiated a migration of immigrant populations from the Lower East Side, who joined the German immigrants that had settled there decades before. (A portrait of the neighborhood in the early twentieth century was immortalized in the classic coming-of-age story *A Tree Grows in Brooklyn*.) In a quirk somewhat out of sync with its melting-pot legacy, many of Williamsburg's streets are named for signers of the Declaration of Independence (including Keap Street, which was an erroneous transliteration of a handwritten document identifying former Pennsylvania governor and Declaration signer Thomas McKean).

This is a large neighborhood by New York City standards, big enough to accommodate several micro-epicenters of aggressively cool commerce. Similar to how in Manhattan numbered streets are designated East or West, the streets in Williamsburg follow a numbered grid, and there is a North side and a South side, divided by Grand Street. The north side, owing to its proximity to the Bedford Avenue subway, was first to gentrify; it's also the more picturesque and more vibrant part. Here, you'll find the developed part of the waterfront, which boasts lush green lawns, perfect Manhattan skyline views, and **Smorgasburg** *(Kent Avenue between North 7th and 8th Streets; www.smorgasburg.com)*, a food lover's paradise that sets up along the waterfront every Saturday.

Though the south side has seen its share of development, it still feels a bit wilder and more disjointed, a vibe that's unlikely to change so long as the Williamsburg Bridge and various roadways chop up the flow on this side of the divide. The south side is where you will find **Peter Luger** *(178 Broadway, between Bedford and Driggs Avenues; www.peterluger.com)*, the legendary steakhouse that predates the bridge by about twenty years. Nearby are **Marlow & Sons** *(81 Broadway, between Wythe Avenue and*

Berry Street; *www.marlowandsons.com*) and **Diner** (*85 Broadway, between Wythe Avenue and Berry Street; www.dinernyc.com*), pioneering restaurants of a different era, whose rise at the turn of the twenty-first century did much to define the Williamsburg (and larger Brooklyn) vibe as any other.

The heart of Williamsburg is the Bedford Avenue L station, which pumps a continuous flow of residents and visitors in and out of Manhattan twenty-four hours a day, seven days a week. But the key to enjoying yourself here is getting away from Bedford Avenue as quickly as possible—it's just too crowded, too stimulating, too much—and one way to do this is to arrive by **ferry** (*www.eastriverferry.com*), which makes stops at Wall Street and East 34th Street in Manhattan, as well as in DUMBO and Greenpoint, in Brooklyn, and Long Island City, in Queens.

Regardless of which method of transportation you take, when you arrive, find your way to one of the streets on the north side that lies between the river and the subway, such as Berry, Wythe, or Kent. Here is where things start to get interesting: old industrial buildings holding storefronts full of handmade treasures, with nary a chain in sight; glass-fronted cafés with hives of stylish worker bees, bathed in the glow of their MacBooks; the Manhattan skyline peeking through the buildings. This part of the neighborhood can feel like the epicenter of a resurgence of American craft: from furniture to chocolate to frilly dresses to pastries so lovingly made their creation is celebrated by an eight-minute video on YouTube, it seems like everything in this neighborhood is handcrafted with love and care out of the finest ingredients. The first must-hit spot on an artisanal-culture walking tour of the north side is **Mast Brothers Chocolate** (*111 North 3rd Street, between Berry Street and Wythe Avenue; www.mastbrothers.com*), an earnest, contemporary version of every child's dream destination. In this chocolate factory, every ingredient and material is thoughtfully sourced, from the cocoa beans that travel from the Dominican Republic to New York by sailboat right down to the patterned paper wrappers in which every bar is carefully placed by hand.

Williamsburg is a terrific place for a romantic evening because, above everything else, it is a destination for beautiful food and drink in memorable spaces. In addition to **Marlow & Sons** and **Diner** (and a few doors down from **Mast Brothers**) is **Egg** (*109 North 3rd Street, between Wythe Avenue and Berry Street; www.eggrestaurant.com*), whose reverently cooked breakfasts—served all day, every day—are a love letter to the foods of the morning hours. (Tip: For the shortest wait, avoid prime weekend brunch hours.) **Isa** (*348 Wythe Avenue, between South 2nd and 3rd Streets; www.isa.gg*) is a bit rowdier, but the cozy, Alpine lodge–inspired decor makes it a particularly ideal destination in the dead of winter. Aim to arrive in time to see the sun set over Manhattan as you walk to the restaurant, and then pull the chill out of your bones with a hot toddy or an excellent pizza from the wood-fired oven. If you prefer more of a wandering date, there is no shortage of cafés and bakeries from which to take your provisions to go. Try **Bakeri** (150 *Wythe Avenue, between North 7th and 8th Streets; www.bakeribrooklyn.com*), where bakers in adorable matching blue jumpsuits provide homemade everything—right down to the hand-churned butter that goes into those delectable croissants.

Though the sunset over Manhattan is indeed a stunner (try the Williamsburg Waterfront, a section of East River State Park that runs along the river), the quintessential Williamsburg date night ends many hours later, at either a music show (there are many live music venues around) or at **Brooklyn Bowl** (61 *Wythe Avenue, between North 11th and 12th Streets; www.brooklynbowl.com*), a LEED-certified bowling alley and music venue with food from the venerable Blue Ribbon. And should you fall so in love with the delicious local culture that you can't bear to cross the water, never fear: Williamsburg's premier boutique hotel, the **Wythe** (80 *Wythe Avenue, between North 11th and 12th Streets; www.wythehotel.com*) lies but a few doors away. There, you can extend your experience in this precious playground by procuring one of the rooms in this converted 1901 factory building, each furnished with locally made furniture and artisanal bath products. Just don't go to your room hungry: though there is an excellent restaurant in the lobby (**Reynard**, from the same owner as Diner and Marlow & Sons), the hotel does not provide room service in an effort to encourage camaraderie between its guests. The Wythe also has a number of rooms suitable for wedding receptions, including two lofts with Manhattan waterfront views (*see page 163*). *Subway: L to Bedford Avenue; J, M to Marcy Avenue.*

PLACES TO SHARE DESSERT

With apologies to oysters and asparagus, it's the final sweet note of a meal that silently and most powerfully invites romance. Couples who conspiratorially stick around at the city's fanciest restaurants for one more course together; or who pull at a shared treat, fingers bumping up against one another as they window-shop in SoHo or along Madison Avenue; or who seek out one of the city's growing number of dessert-only tasting menus know that, when kindling romance, it helps to lay on the sweet.

BROOKLYN FARMACY. Nostalgia has its advantages, and the Brooklyn Farmacy & Soda Fountain is one of them. Tucked away on Henry Street in Carroll Gardens, this is the kind of ice cream parlor your grandparents might recognize from the old days, with gold frosted letters on the windows, a long bar with tables around it, and a menu of shakes and sundaes that would give pause to even the most decisive appetite. They do serve a range of comforting savory plates—from indulgent egg dishes at brunch to classic deli sandwiches like the Cuban and the pastrami at lunch, and of course a beloved grilled cheese—but the real reason to go here is for the ice cream. Leave time after a meal anywhere in the neighborhood, and come here to dip straws into either side of a giant sundae (with extra hot fudge, of course). *513 Henry Street, between Sackett and Union Streets, in Brooklyn. 718-522-6260. www.brooklynfarmacy.blogspot.com. Subway: F, G to Carroll Street.*

CAFÉ SABARSKY. This incredibly appealing, transporting café is located in the **Neue Galerie**, the wonderful German–Austrian art museum on the Upper East Side. The restaurant is designed like a traditional Viennese coffeehouse, but even if you have never been to Austria, the wood-and-glass-paneled interior with curvy metal chairs and beautiful glass display cases will conjure up something special and European. The restaurant serves breakfast, lunch, and dinner, but the real stars here are the coffee and desserts. In traditional coffeehouse style, patrons are welcome (and even encouraged) to linger over *kaffee*s and a single, decadent slice of cake (*mit Schlag*, of course) for as long as they like. Viennese confections such as Linzer torte, apple strudel, and Sacher torte are presented on a marble-topped mantel across one of the café's walls; on the other side, sunlight pours in through windows overlooking Central Park. Café Sabarsky is ideal for a late-afternoon sweet, the hour when a couple can steal away for the type of treat that threatens to ruin an appetite. *N.B.:* The café is not open on Tuesdays, when the museum is closed. *1048 Fifth Avenue, between East 85th and 86th Streets in Manhattan. 212-288-0665. www.neuegalerie.org/cafes/sabarsky. Subway: 4, 5, 6 to 86th Street.*

CHIKALICIOUS. Sometimes when you are looking forward to a restaurant's dessert, you have to have the discipline to order a light dinner. However, if your evening plans involve ChikaLicious, you can forgo the prelude altogether. This jewel box of a restaurant offers simply a short list of incredibly attractive seasonal desserts or, as they put it, "American desserts, French presentation, and Japanese tasting portions." The $16 prix fixe includes an amuse-bouche, petits fours, and a choice of one dessert plate. (A wine pairing is available for an additional $8.) ChikaLicious does not accept reservations, so go early or late to avoid a wait for two of the twenty seats. And while we entirely recommend partaking in the full experience, if you are pressed for time, ChikaLicious has a to-go operation called Dessert Club, right across the street. *203 East 10th Street, between First and Second Avenues, in Manhattan. 212-475-0929. www.chikalicious.com. Subway: L to First Avenue or Third Avenue; 6 to Astor Place.*

MOMOFUKU MILK BAR. Dotted around the city like candles in a birthday cake, the Momofuku Milk Bars are great spots for an indulgent treat. Celebrated for their truffle cakes and cereal milk (which is exactly what it sounds like), the Milk Bars also make the most heart-stoppingly sweet and delicious cookies around (from the compost cookie, which is a mixture of everything you might ever want to put in a chocolate chip cookie to model Karlie Kloss's gluten-free "kookies"), slices of addictively sweet pies, and soft-serve ice cream and milkshakes in flavors that will awaken your inner child. With locations uptown, in midtown, downtown, and in Brooklyn, you're never too far from a tasty way to wrap up an evening on a whim. *Locations across the city. Check www.milkbarstore.com for details.*

ONCE UPON A TART. A day of shopping and sightseeing in SoHo can be hard on the feet and the wallet. So when your belly is crying out for sustenance and your credit card is ready to say uncle, wander west a bit away from the fray, and then migrate up a block to this dimly lit, off-the-radar café on Sullivan Street. Once Upon a Tart looks like it belongs on a Parisian side street (and the cozy surrounding block supports that image), and when you walk inside, the intense, power-shopping atmosphere of SoHo will indeed feel 5,000 miles away. Per their name, tarts—both sweet and savory—are the specialty (though soups, sandwiches, salads, and pastries are offered as well). Tarts are individually sized, but sharing is fine, too, if you are so inclined. *135 Sullivan Street, between Houston and Prince Streets, in Manhattan. 212-387-8869. www. onceuponatart.com. Subway: 1 to Houston Street; C, E to Spring Street; N, R to Prince Street.*

PER SE. The swankiest New York City dessert date is at Per Se, Thomas Keller's lauded Time Warner Center restaurant. Utterly impossible to take a full meal at without advance planning and a full bank account, Per Se has, as of late, added a special dessert-only tasting menu that is available in the salon, the restaurant's no-reservation dining area. You could order any one of the nightly desserts à la carte there, but we suggest indulging in the exquisite decadence of the full five-course tasting menu to really experience this temple of edible delicacy. Offerings change nightly and reflect both the seasons and the restaurant's signature wizardry with food that has made it world-famous. Tables in the salon are snapped up quickly during prime dining hours, so we suggest making this a late-night stop (perhaps after a show at Jazz at Lincoln Center, which is downstairs?), when you and your date will have the intimacy and leisure to enjoy this spectacular dining experience. *10 Columbus Circle, between West 58th and 60th Streets, in Manhattan. 212-823-9335. www.perseny.com. Subway: A, B, C, D, 1 to 59th Street–Columbus Circle.*

FIREPLACES TO GET COZY BY

In this progressive age of technological dependency and energy-efficient bulbs, there's something heartwarming about discovering those places where candlelight and fireplaces are still allowed to bring warmth and light the old-fashioned way. Maybe it's the soft, flickering light, and maybe it's the soporific effect of all those naked flames in a small room. But somehow the presence of a fireplace draws a room in around it and turns a tiny spot into a cozy one—and any evening into a romantic one. These days, real fireplaces are few and far between in this city; these are some of our favorites.

BLACK MOUNTAIN WINE HOUSE. This Brooklyn wine bar is decorated like an upstate cabin, complete with a cluster of Adirondack chairs that welcome you to its gated front patio. But on chilly nights, you'll want to take a glass of a bracing red and huddle close to the fireplace. The food menu changes daily, and all plates are modestly priced (cuddling to get toasty in front of the hearth is available at no additional charge). *415 Union Street, between Hoyt and Bond Streets, in Brooklyn. www.blackmountainwinehouse. com. Subway: F, G to Carroll Street.*

THE NOMAD. There is no shortage of good reasons to visit the restaurant inside the NoMad Hotel: the gorgeous atrium, which makes even the most raw winter day feel warm and springlike; the food at the restaurant from the men who earned three Michelin stars at Eleven Madison Park; the exquisite old-fashioned dessert cart, from which you can select your pastry after getting a good look at all of the day's offerings; and the rooftop private dining room, with its gorgeous skyscraper views, that can be booked for weddings *(see page 163)*. Add to this list the restaurant's hidden gem, the fireplace room, a semiprivate area away from the main dining room, where you and a beloved can enjoy a hearth-lit meal courtesy of an antique marble fireplace imported from a French château. The fireplace room contains only six tables, making it the perfect setting for a proposal, an anniversary, or a quiet seduction hidden from prying eyes. **N.B.:** Reservations are recommended, and to sit in the fireplace room, you are encouraged to request it at the time of booking. *Located inside the NoMad Hotel at 1170 Broadway, between West 27th and 28th Streets, in Manhattan. 212-796-1500. www. thenomadhotel.com. Subway: N, R to 28th Street.*

EMPLOYEES ONLY. Tucked into a relatively quiet stretch of Hudson Street in the West Village, Employees Only is known first for its cocktail list, a collection of contemporary interpretations of classics designed to complement an equally fragrant hearty French menu. But the jewel in its crown of an art deco interior is the steel-fronted fireplace, which gives the place an old-fashioned, unpredictable heat and lends a seductive flicker to everything in the room, from the mirrored shelves of liquor behind the bar to the warm wood tabletops. Get a table near the fireplace and you'll find a cozy drink evolves nicely into a romantic meal. *510 Hudson Street between Christopher and West 10th Streets, in Manhattan. 212-242-3021. www.employeesonlynyc.com. Subway: 1 to Christopher Street–Sheridan Square; A, B, C, D, E, F, M to West 4th Street.*

CLOVER CLUB. In among the hubbub of Smith Street, on the border between the busy neighborhoods of Boerum Hill and Carroll Gardens, Clover Club is a grand throwback to the classic cocktail bars of the 1920s. At the far end of one of the longest bars in all of Brooklyn, the adventurous among you can push through to a semi-hidden back room where, in the cooler months, a cozier bar area glows in the warmth of a large corner fireplace. Settle in on the couch and give your bartender a few hints at your palate, and their creative mixologists will do the rest. With an award-winning list of drinks and equally inventive mocktails, this is a great place to end a romantic evening. (We'd say it's a wonderful place to begin one, too, but after a couple of drinks by the fireside here you won't want to go anywhere but home.) *210 Smith Street, between Butler and Baltic Streets, in Brooklyn. 718-855-7939. www.cloverclubny. com. Subway: F, G to Bergen Street.*

ALTA. A hidden gem on the eastern side of the West Village, Alta is an authentic Spanish hacienda hidden inside an old brick townhouse. People come for the food—an elaborate and innovative menu of tapas and small plates that range from light salads and fresh seafood to delicious grilled vegetables and rich meats and pâtés—but stay for the atmosphere, which is equal parts lively and intimate. A large wood fireplace crackles at the end of the main dining room but casts enough warmth to be felt by the diners on the balcony floor upstairs. Call to reserve the table immediately in front of the fire—it's worth planning ahead for. *64 West 10th Street, between Fifth and Sixth Avenues, in Manhattan. 212-505-7777. www.altarestaurant.com. Subway: A, B, C, D, E, F, M to West 4th Street.*

DINING ALFRESCO

Each spring, as soon as the temperature reaches "tolerable," New Yorkers flock en masse to sidewalk cafés and restaurant gardens. Dining outdoors is something of a local tradition, evidenced by the lengths restaurant owners will go to secure a license for a little piece of sidewalk on which to throw out a small outdoor table or two. Plopping down at any sidewalk café you stumble on has a certain urban charm, but those who want more romance, discretion, and intimacy should seek out a restaurant with a garden, such as the ones below.

CANNIBAL. The area east of Madison Square Park is not the most obvious destination for romantic garden spots, filled as it is with office buildings and skyscrapers. But tucked into one of the side streets is a diamond in the rough in the form of a meat-centric restaurant run by Belgian cycling enthusiasts and named for the famous Belgian bicyclist Eddy "The Cannibal" Merckx. Given its unlikely surroundings, Cannibal's garden seems all the more an endearing oasis, a pleasant spot nicely shaded by surrounding buildings and trees and filled with picnic tables, plants, and shrubs, with strings of lights crisscrossing overhead. A number of the entrées are designed to be shared by two, so a pair of carnivorous lovebirds can feast on the steak du jour or a slow-roasted half of a pig's head. Cannibal can be lively on weeknights, although the garden is always more subdued (and if it's quiet you are after, you should avoid making your visit while the Tour de France is on). *113 East 29th Street, between Lexington Avenue and Park Avenue South, in Manhattan. 212-686-5480. www.cannibalnyc.com. Subway: 6 to 28th Street.*

FRANKIES 457. Now something of a miniature local empire, with outposts in Brooklyn and the West Village, the Frankies restaurants are known for their authentic and expressive take on home-cooked Italian and Spanish food. But this restaurant, on Court Street, was the first—and it has a beautiful large garden, too. Step down from the restaurant's back door and take a seat under the canopy, surrounded by plants and trees and honeysuckle, and enjoy some amazing pasta and meat dishes the way they would be enjoyed in the old country. *457 Court Street, between 4th Place and Luquer Street, in Brooklyn. 718-403-0033. www.frankiesspuntino.com. Subway: F, G to Carroll Street.*

LAVENDER LAKE. Taking its name from the ironic moniker once given to the neighborhood's famously flavorful canal, this charming bar and restaurant in Gowanus has one of the cutest outdoor spaces in all of Brooklyn. Hidden among the largely industrial blocks on either side of the canal, the garden is nicely defined by weathered wooden decking and simple furniture and seems to float in a quiet and semisecret space between the canal and the low buildings that surround it. It's good for hot wine and cider in the fall, and perfect for brunch and drinks in the warmer months. *383 Carroll Street, between Bond and Nevins Streets, in Brooklyn. 347-799-2154. www.lavenderlake. com. Subway: R to Union Street; F, G to Carroll Street.*

MAISON PREMIERE. Attentively designed to capture the look and spirit of a century-old French absinthe bar—even down to the bronze Napoleon statue atop the taps—Maison Premiere is something of an enigma on Bedford Avenue. Popular for indulgent racks of oysters and other shellfish, and for a cocktail list that rejuvenates old classics (often with the help of the aforementioned absinthe), it's a small and intimate place with only a few tables, making it good for a champagne-and-oyster date or a quiet drink. The covered garden that opens out to the back is a lush, Mediterranean-inspired space with a glass roof and a conservatory feel, and it's draped in vines and other greenery—the perfect environment for a decadent evening. *298 Bedford Avenue, between Grand and South 1st Streets, in Brooklyn. 347-335-0446. www.maisonpremiere.com. Subway: L to Bedford Avenue; J, M to Marcy Avenue.*

MARCHI'S. One of the oldest restaurants in Manhattan's quiet Murray Hill neighborhood, Marchi's is a memory of a former age that somehow endures. An old-school Italian restaurant, there is famously no menu here—you show up to a fairly anonymous brownstone, are invited in, and sit down to several courses of traditional hearty northern Italian food. The inside dining rooms are almost oppressive, but go in spring or summer and sit outside in one of the most surprising gardens in the city. Overwhelmingly lush, with a large old tree in its center and flowers and plants and herbs growing along its walls and in pots scattered among the tables, it's a breath of fresh air and an experience worth waiting for. *251 East 31st Street, between Second and Third Avenues, in Manhattan. 212-679-2494. www.marchirestaurant. com. Subway: 6 to 28th Street or 33rd Street.*

PURE FOOD AND WINE. With real estate always at a premium, it's rare to find a restaurant garden that is large enough to eat in without worrying about getting your elbow in someone else's plate. The great luxury of the backyard of this Irving Place restaurant is how spacious it is. There are a few dozen tables, and it's lined with a long, upholstered banquette on one side and a bar on the other. Pure is an upscale raw vegan restaurant, and the plates are dazzling compositions of colorful produce. If this kind of food doesn't immediately draw you over for a romantic meal, perhaps this detail will: it was at this restaurant that Alec Baldwin presented his business card to future wife Hilaria Thomas, after spotting her eating at a separate table across the room. *54 Irving Place, between East 17th and 18th Streets, in Manhattan. 212-477-1010. www. oneluckyduck.com. Subway: 4, 5, 6, L, N, Q, R to 14th Street–Union Square.*

VINEGAR HILL HOUSE. Deep in Vinegar Hill, the quiet and bewitchingly colonial-looking residential neighborhood that borders DUMBO, is hidden one of the gems of Brooklyn. Vinegar Hill House is a fantastic restaurant, with a rich and creative menu of French and American cuisine and a warm and cozy candlelit atmosphere that its popularity doesn't seem to dampen. The real treat, though, is getting a table in the garden: enclosed by old brick walls, with the houses of Vinegar Hill opening to the sky above and leafy trees bowing over the tables, it feels like you're having dinner in a friend's backyard. *72 Hudson Avenue, between Front and Water Streets, in Brooklyn. 718-522-1018. www.vinegarhillhouse.com. Subway: F to York Street; A, C to High Street.*

SHH! IT'S A SECRET

Underground, unmarked, and misleading: this combination might not seem like the recipe for a good business plan in a city where restaurants rely on foot traffic. Somehow, some cocktail nooks and secret restaurants manage to survive and thrive here, because of their discreet presence rather than in spite of it.

HUDSON CLEARWATER. The secret about this West Village restaurant is that it isn't where it says it is; arrive at 447 Hudson Street, and you'll find a boarded-up storefront. Not to worry. Simply walk around the corner and enter the green garden door, through which you'll find a charming patio filled, most likely, with beautiful Villagers sipping cocktails. Keep on walking through the back door and you'll reach the small L-shaped dining room, a transporting journey that eases the transition from Manhattan street to cozy respite. It's not hard to imagine you have

DO YOU RIDE THE TRAIN?

Apologies to fans of Select Bus Service and devotees of the crosstown routes, but the sexiest mode of transit in the MTA's arsenal is without a doubt the subway. And you know how the phrase goes: the couple that rides the subway together stays together. Here, our selection of preferred routes.

L. The L travels through several neighborhoods populated by hip young people— Greenpoint and Williamsburg, in Brooklyn, the East Village, and Chelsea—which accounts for the prettiness factor of its ridership. L riders put work into their image, and it shows.

A and D. The sex appeal of the A and the D come not from their ridership, but from the style of their routes. Both trains whisk passengers between West 59th and 125th Streets without stopping, jetting through the Upper West Side with unparalleled insouciance. These express trains are for New Yorkers who know their business.

G. A short train with an unpredictable schedule and a small but loyal team of subscribers, the G is the subway equivalent of being a regular at an obscure, old-school neighborhood bar. If you're one of the crowd—a mix of Brooklyn and Queens neighborhoods, with hipsters from Greenpoint to Red Hook—the seats will start to feel like your favorite booth in the back.

N, Q, and B. Ride with someone special, and in the moment the train emerges onto the Manhattan Bridge from the tunnel, you can profess your love against the backdrop of the New York City skyline.

---

stumbled upon a dimly lit tavern in some out-of-the-way country town, especially once you try one of the elegant cocktails named in honor of local regions ("Upstate Rose"; "Kings County") in hand. Stick with the local theme by moving on to a wine from the Finger Lakes or Long Island, and then dig in to earnest farm-to-table dishes like crispy duck breast, braised pork, or mushroom-accented farro. Hudson Clearwater is open for brunch, lunch, dinner, and drinks; it's the perfect place to seek out after an afternoon of wandering around the **West Village** (*see page 53*). *447 Hudson Street, between Morton and Barrow Streets (enter around the corner on Morton Street), in Manhattan. 212-989-3255. www.hudsonclearwater.com. Subway: 1 to Christopher Street or Houston Street.*

PDT. PDT stands for Please Don't Tell, which gives a hint to the atmosphere this hidden East Village drinking den wants to convey. Truth be told, the existence of PDT isn't much of a secret anymore (it's been around for seven years), but the experience will always have a clandestine feel, thanks to its idiosyncratic location inside of Crif Dogs, a hot dog joint. When you arrive in the evening, join the short queue alongside Crif's vintage arcade games. When it's your turn, pick up the receiver inside the vintage phone booth and give your name. A hidden door will then be opened, and you will be led to a table for two in the dimly lit bar that has magically appeared before you. Cocktails are the order of the evening, and all drinks on the menu are prepared with painterly attentiveness to color and balance. Requests for simpler drinks (as well as nonalcoholic concoctions) are taken as well. And here, no mere tray of peanuts will do; should you become peckish during your time imbibing, you may complement your highball in only-in-New-York fashion by ordering a hot dog, a burger, fries, or tater tots from next door. **N.B.:** Reservations are recommended, especially on weekends. *113 St. Marks Place, between First Avenue and Avenue A, in Manhattan. 212-614-0386. www.pdtnyc.com. Subway: L to First Avenue or 6 to Astor Place.*

SAKAGURA. There is virtually no way you will stumble upon this underground Japanese restaurant, which is on a nondescript midtown block and virtually unmarked, save for a small red sign above the doorway of the office building it lies within. To access this well-hidden gem, you must pass the doorman, enter the emergency stairwell, and descend to the basement. There you will find one of the most romantic restaurants in the city and one of the premier sake destinations in the United States. The lovely bar and dining room are decorated with shoji screens and live plants, and although Sakagura is smack in the middle of a business center and Grand Central Terminal, the serenity of the atmosphere is further enhanced by the lack of cellular reception. Sakagura is open for lunch, but it's nicer at dinner, when the suits have gone and are replaced by couples lingering over cocktails and *omakase*. The sake list is as long as a pillow book, but your server can guide you through and offer suggestions for pairings. **N.B.:** Reservations are recommended for dinner. *211 East 43rd Street, between Second and Third Avenues, in Manhattan. 212-953-7253. www. sakagura.com. Subway: 4, 5, 6, 7 to Grand Central–42nd Street.*

THE TIPPLER. The Tippler inhabits an underground space in a building with a long history in the local appetizer business. This bar is located beneath Chelsea Market, an upscale food court that was formerly the Nabisco cookie factory, and unlike in the market, many of the architectural details in the Tippler make reference to the space's earlier industrial history. Decorated with an eclectic mix of brick, tile, wrought iron, oriental rugs, and marble, the bar hits the nostalgia key hard, though the cocktail list (which is mercifully concise compared to other bars of this ilk) features some modern interpretations of classic drinks. There is also a short menu of civilized bar eats (shrimp cocktail, tartines, and simple salads). Ideal for an afternoon cocktail or quick early evening bite (late nights on weekends suffer from Meatpacking District nightlife spillover), the Tippler is perfectly positioned to greet you after a walk across the **High Line** or an afternoon of **gallery hopping** (*see page 50*). *425 West 15th Street, between Ninth and Tenth Avenues, in Manhattan. 212-206-0000. www. thetippler.com. Subway: A, C, E to 14th Street; L to Eighth Avenue.*

RAINES LAW ROOM. It sounds like a place where a budding Juris Doctor might cram for the bar exam, but in actuality, this is a sexy cocktail den full of unexpected nooks concealed from onlookers by curtains, perfect for a clandestine tipple just for two. (The Raines Law was the 1896 prohibition on Sunday liquor sales in New York.) When you arrive at No. 48, press the bell, and a smartly dressed host will open the door and let you know if there is room for your party. (Tip: Try to arrive before 5:30 p.m. on Thursdays, Fridays, and Saturdays, or make a reservation for your preferred time on Sundays, Mondays, or Tuesdays.) You may be led to a Chesterfield sofa in the lounge, a velvet-covered banquette in the parlor, or into the charming garden, which also provides herbs and berries featured on the extensive cocktail menu. In further pursuit of intimacy, servers can be beckoned (or not) with the ring of a buzzer. *48 West 17th Street, between Fifth and Sixth Avenues, in Manhattan. No phone. www.raineslawroom. com. Subway: F, M to 14th Street; L to Sixth Avenue; 1 to 18th Street.*

LITTLE BRANCH. People could walk around the West Village for years and never realize that the unassuming and unmarked door on the corner of Seventh Avenue and Leroy Street leads to one of the most seductive watering holes in the city. A sibling establishment of the pioneering secret cocktail bar Milk & Honey, Little Branch is as well suited to a first date as it is to a twentieth-anniversary celebration. A beautiful room paneled in vintage decor, topped with a pressed-tin ceiling, and lined with booths that are perfect for two, Little Branch is as nice to look at as it is pleasant to sit in. The bartenders here are serious about what they do, but also remarkably accommodating—explain what you like, and they'll offer you a range of delicious drinks to suit and find custom-carved chunks of ice to fit every kind of tumbler. It's an ideal place for a predinner drink or two—and nothing beats emerging back onto the street corner through the anonymity of the unmarked door, the rest of the Village none the wiser. *20 Seventh Avenue South, between Leroy and Clarkson Streets, in Manhattan. 212-929-4360. Subway: 1 to Houston Street; B, C, D, E, F, M to West 4th Street.*

BOHEMIAN. Secret doesn't come much more secret than this. Whether you're in town for a week's vacation or you've lived here for a decade, this hidden Japanese restaurant is one of the city's greatest surprises and worth taking someone special to. Beyond the immaculate storefront of a specialist Japanese butcher in NoHo sits the unmarked and little-known Bohemian—a small restaurant and bar with room for about twenty-five lucky diners and only two or three sittings a night. True to its neighbor out front, Bohemian's menu features some of the finest cuts of steak in the city, as well as a range of imaginative dishes that include Japanese specialties like sea urchin or beef sashimi and traditional American bar fare with a twist, such as the Wagyu beef sliders. The food is impressive, but it's the atmosphere and the secrecy of the whole affair that make Bohemian so much fun. Be advised: after you track down the phone number, you still have to book long in advance—so this is the kind of surprise you need to plan ahead for. *57 Great Jones Street, between Lafayette Street and Bowery, in Manhattan. www.playearth.jp. Subway: B, D, F, M to Broadway–Lafayette Street; 6 to Bleecker Street.*

CHAPTER 3

GETTING SERIOUS WITH THE CITY

Nora Ephron, in whose vision of romance New York City was oft the shimmering backdrop, once said that after a year of living elsewhere, she decided she could never live anywhere but New York. For her, regular life felt mundane after spending so long in "the most exciting, magical, fraught-with-possibility place that you could ever live in." To Ephron and many of her fellow New Yorkers, the city's natural propensity for elevating ordinary or personal activities to experiences that feel epic and exceptional is one of its most alluring features. (Not having to eke through daily hours in a car is not far behind.) The multisensory fabric of the city—the sights, tastes, and sounds of our diverse megalopolis—seeps into every outing, errand, and, yes, romantic date.

In the spirit of marrying the private joys of courtship anywhere to city-specific wonder, in this chapter, we take two activities—dating and sightseeing—each alluring in its own right, and unite them to create local itineraries that give you and your beloved the best of both: ideas for how to see great, notable parts of the city in fresh, romantically tinged ways; and, conversely, suggestions for how to imbue traditional date activities with that "exciting, magical, fraught-with-possibility" energy that Ephron missed while on her sabbatical.

DINNER AND A MOVIE?

Pretty much anywhere in the Western world, the mere suggestion of a date inspires in everybody the same first association: dinner and a movie. No other city offers as many variations on this time-honored progression from silverware to the silver screen than New York.

Anyone can play it safe with a New York slice of pizza and a blockbuster at the Regal in Union Square. But in a city with more movie theaters and restaurants per square mile than almost anywhere in the world, you can afford to think outside the box (office) a little. Get to know the city's neighborhoods and you'll find that culture and cuisine often go hand in hand, with the grander cinemas a mere doorman's whistle away from fine dining, and the art-house theaters a flicked cigarette's flight from the hip restaurants du jour.

With that in mind, here are five suggestions for romantic evenings that take dinner and a movie and give it a local twist—each with an appropriate venue for post-movie arguments and kisses.

Prune, Sunshine, and Il Laboratorio del Gelato

Prune, the Landmark Sunshine theater, and Il Laboratorio del Gelato are three diamonds in the relative rough of East Houston Street. Small, lively, and always busy, Prune *(54 East 1st Street, between First and Second Avenue, in Manhattan; www.prunerestaurant.com)* is adventurous French and American cuisine masquerading as an informal café—a fun spot to be private among the pleasant downtown rabble. The **Sunshine** *(143 East Houston Street, between Forsyth and Eldridge Streets, in Manhattan; www.landmarktheatres.com)*, a beautifully restored old theater, runs a good program of movies, with one foot in the mainstream and the other in European art house. And you can follow it all with the creamiest gelato in the city, from **Il Laboratorio's** *(188 Ludlow Street, between Stanton and East Houston Streets, in Manhattan; www.laboratoriodelgelato. com)* sparse and minimal industrial space. *Subway: F to Second Avenue.*

Frankies Spuntino, Cobble Hill Cinema, and Brooklyn Social

With a hearty Italian menu, an adorable backyard, and a cozy and friendly inside, **Frankies Spuntino** *(457 Court Street, between 4th Place and Luquer Street, in Brooklyn; www.frankiesspuntino.com)* is one of Carroll Gardens' best-loved restaurants and most charming dinner-date spots. A pleasant stroll down Court Street, the **Cobble Hill Cinemas** *(265 Court Street, between Butler and Douglass Streets, in Brooklyn; www.cobblehilltheatre.com)*, with painted vignettes of classics adorning the weathered townhouse walls outside, is one of the sweetest old neighborhood theaters in "rejuvenated" Brooklyn. And to complete a nostalgic evening, argue over the movie at **Brooklyn Social** *(335 Smith Street, between President and Carroll Streets, in Brooklyn; www.brooklynsocialbar.com)*, the quiet-looking old-school cocktail bar tucked away at the Carroll Gardens end of Smith Street, where the drinks are strong, couples fill the booths, and the watchful eyes of old Brooklynites stare down from photos on the wall. *Subway: F, G to Carroll Street.*

The Planetarium, Shake Shack, and Central Park

Whisk your date into the latest showing of the **Hayden Planetarium's** *(Central Park West at West 79th Street, in Manhattan; www.haydenplanetarium.org)* perennially

entertaining *Journey to the Stars*, which affords the same opportunities to sit closely and whisper in the darkness as any movie theater, as well as the innocent charm of an unusually glamorous field trip. Then pick up the best burgers and shakes the city has to offer at **Shake Shack** *(366 Columbus Avenue, between West 77th and 78th Streets, in Manhattan; www.shakeshack.com)*, walk over to the park, eat them in the light of dusk, and see if you can pick out any constellations. *Subway: B, C to 81st Street–Museum of Natural History.*

Bar Boulud, Lincoln Center Plaza, and the Mandarin Oriental

For the upscale date, head uptown. **Bar Boulud** *(1900 Broadway, between West 63rd and 64th Streets, in Manhattan; www.barboulud.com)* is the most accessible and affordable of Daniel Boulud's city eateries, and one of the only high-end restaurants uptown that can cater to the theatergoing crowd (and understand the importance of getting the check on time). **Lincoln Center** *(1941 Broadway, between West 65th and 66th Streets, in Manhattan; lc.lincolncenter.org)* is one of the city's fairy-tale date spots, a cultural wonderland lit up by the lights of the various halls and the fountain in the center of the plaza. Take in a movie at Alice Tully Hall, which is fancy enough that they host the New York Film Festival here; then head down along Central Park West to the bar at the **Mandarin Oriental** *(80 Columbus Circle, between West 58th and 60th Streets, in Manhattan; www.mandarinoriental.com)*, where you and your date can sip colorful cocktails and look out over the park and the fountains of Columbus Circle. *Subway: 1 to 66th Street–Lincoln Center.*

Peninsula Hotel, Paris Theatre, and the Pulitzer Fountain

For those who believe in the enduring allure of the classics, this is the date for you. **The Peninsula** *(700 Fifth Avenue, between West 54th and 55th Streets, in Manhattan; www. peninsula.com)* is one of midtown's hidden gems, a beautiful old hotel off Fifth Avenue with a sophisticated restaurant inside and a rooftop bar that lets you look up and down the city, from the windows of Tiffany & Co. to Museum Mile. **The Paris** *(4 West 58th Street, between Fifth and Sixth Avenues, in Manhattan; www.theparistheatre.com)* is the only theater that can match the Peninsula for old-world class; dress your best and make sure to arrive on time so you can watch the velvet curtain rise before showtime. After the movie, walk across the street to the square outside the Plaza Hotel to discuss the film you've just seen in front of the Pulitzer Fountain. Test your date's cinematic knowledge by asking what classic romantic movie ends in this spot (*The Way We Were*), and give him or her bonus points for remembering the closing line. ("Your girl

The marquee of the Paris Theater

is lovely, Hubble.") If you're feeling peckish, duck into **The Plaza Food Hall** (*1 West 59th Street, between Fifth and Sixth Avenues, in Manhattan; www.theplazany.com*), where you can pick up a snack or treat to go from one of the vendors. Our suggestion: a traditional black-and-white cookie from William Greenberg Desserts, a Manhattan bakery that's been around since the '40s. *Subway: E, M to Fifth Avenue–53rd Street; F to 57th Street; N, Q, R to Fifth Avenue–59th Street.*

OUT AND ABOUT

The ability to walk all around New York is what makes the city different from most of America—this is a place of beautiful parks and small neighborhoods, built for people to get around on foot. It's also what allies New York more closely to the great cities of Europe and Asia and what makes being here so engaging. A walk on a nice afternoon can make for a lovely and unassuming date, and there is so much to see in New York that you can't go wrong. Our best advice is to make sure you have an end point in the back of your mind, so you can impress your date by pointing out the perfect charming café at the end of a long day's wander.

BRIDGING THE GAP

Hart Crane, one of America's great poets and one of New York's greatest admirers, wrote of "the ecstasy of walking hand in hand across the most beautiful bridge of the world." He was referring to the **Brooklyn Bridge**, whose beauty and might continue to make the same impression to this day. It's certainly still the city's most attractive bridge, and by virtue of being the southernmost bridge leaving Manhattan, it also has the least obstructed views of New York Harbor, Governors Island, and Staten Island beyond.

The beauty of the bridge-strolling date is that you can start from either side and finish with something great. Meet in Manhattan in the beautiful **City Hall Park** (*Chambers Street at Centre Street*), walk over the bridge to Brooklyn to work up an appetite, and then find solace in the legendary **Grimaldi's** pizza (*1 Front Street, between Old Fulton and Dock Streets, in Brooklyn; www.grimaldisnyc.com*) or a scoop or two from the **Brooklyn Ice Cream Factory** (*1 Water Street, at Brooklyn Bridge Park, in Brooklyn; www.brooklynicecreamfactory.com*), which is the sweeter outpost of the **River Café** (*1 Water Street, at Brooklyn Bridge Park, in Brooklyn; www.rivercafe.com*) alongside it on the waterfront. *The Manhattan side of the bridge starts at City Hall. Subway: 4, 5, 6 to Brooklyn Bridge–City Hall.*

Go the other way, and you can meet by the gloriously restored **carousel** *(Old Dock Street, at the East River, in Brooklyn; www.janescarousel.com)* in DUMBO's beautiful **Brooklyn Bridge Park** and walk over the bridge to Manhattan—and then take your pick between a short walk north through a quiet stretch of historic buildings around the New York Stock Exchange into **Chinatown** for dinner or a quick dive south into the labyrinth of the **Financial District** for drinks in some of the oldest watering holes in the city. *The Brooklyn side of the bridge starts at Adams and Tillary Streets. Subway: A, C to High Street; 2, 3 to Clark Street.*

THE BROOKLYN "RIVIERA"

Much is made of the great romantic rivieras of Europe. Everybody remembers Audrey Hepburn drifting slowly down the Seine with Cary Grant in *Charade*, or indeed dancing after dark beside the Tiber with Gregory Peck in *Roman Holiday*. Well, New York's waterfronts are every bit as sexy and romantic as their European counterparts, from Woody and Diane's sunrise over the East River in *Manhattan* to Mickey Rourke and Kim Basinger in a houseboat on the Hudson in *9½ Weeks*.

Brooklyn's seafront runs from Coney Island on the southeastern corner along the southern shore to Manhattan Beach, in Brooklyn, and Rockaway, in Queens—a relatively short stretch that nonetheless manages to encompass some of the liveliest, most eccentric, and most enjoyable parts of the city. Only the very bravest should contemplate spending a day there out of season, when the icy wind whips in off the Atlantic and the boardwalk is damp with ocean spray, but in spring and summer, an afternoon at the beach can be a wonderful reminder that there is more to the city than concrete and glass. It's the perfect excuse to spend a few hours walking and talking with someone without a table between you.

We suggest you meet at the hub of it all—**Nathan's Hot Dogs** *(1310 Surf Avenue, between West 15th Street and Stillwell Avenue, in Brooklyn; www.nathansfamous.com)* at Coney Island, just a couple of minutes' walk from the subway and in the backyard of Astroland, the once-great amusement park. Next door to Nathan's is **Williams Candy** *(1318 Surf Avenue, between West 15th Street and Stillwell Avenue, in Brooklyn; www.candytreats.com)*, longtime purveyors of such staples of beach fare as toffee apples and cotton candy. Here, you can indulge in a little shameless carbo-loading and pick up something sweet to fuel your walk on the waterfront.

The **Brooklyn boardwalk** is one of the longest in America, and somehow—whether it's the feel of the wood beneath your feet, the smell of the fresh sea air, or the slow-moving old Russian couples strolling arm in arm—it still feels like it must've felt when it opened nearly a century ago. If you head east from Coney Island, you need do nothing but follow the planks underfoot to take in such wonderful distractions as the **Cyclone** roller coaster *(Surf Avenue, between West 10th and 12th Streets, in Brooklyn; www.lunaparknyc.com)*, the **New York Aquarium** *(602 Surf Avenue, at West 8th Street, in Brooklyn; www.nyaquarium.com)*, and the **Russian tearooms** at Brighton Beach—and always with beautiful views of the Atlantic stretching out to the horizon along the way.

If all goes well and the fun keeps you going through Brighton Beach, we suggest you end the afternoon at **Papa Leone's** pizzeria *(103 Oriental Boulevard, between West End Avenue and Amherst Street, in Brooklyn; 718-648-1349)* at Manhattan Beach—one of the last true family-run Italian pizza joints left in the quietest beachfront neighborhood. Time it right, and your (slower) walk back to Coney Island for the train ride home will be at dusk, so you can see the lights of the New Jersey coast flickering and reflecting in the ocean. *Subway: D, F, N, Q to Coney Island–Stillwell Avenue.*

LANDMARK EXPEDITIONS

With due respect to the traditional modes of sightseeing—arrive at attraction, view said attraction, move on to the next one—that's not the only way to see our city. Given the number of diverse things to visit, experience, taste, and partake in, it's possible and utterly enjoyable to enhance the act of sightseeing (particularly if you've visited New York before) by crafting full-day or half-day itineraries around a location or theme, and by reenvisioning the experience of our most famed landmarks by changing the vantage point. The uniting thread of the activities described below— from spending hours poring over the layers of history at Grand Central, to visiting the American Museum of Natural History for the express purpose of seeing their origami tree, to getting up close and personal with Lady Liberty from the water—is that they highlight specific or novel ways to see some of our famous sites and are more date-worthy propositions than simply visiting each attraction on its own.

FUN IN GRAND CENTRAL

Grand Central Terminal has all the components of a good date (food, drink, entertainment) and is centrally located, housed in a building that drips with old New York glamour. The famous Beaux-Arts structure (which turned one hundred in 2013) is a magnificent celebration of the steam, steel, and power that launched New York City to the forefront of travel technology in the early twentieth century. Today, its marble

Grand Central's Main Concourse, with the information booth and its famous clock in the center

floors are traversed by more than 500,000 people every day, and it's one of the most popular tourist destinations in the world. But Grand Central Terminal (only the subway portion is Grand Central Station) has a number of elegant and secret pleasures that make it perhaps the most bustling intimate setting in the world.

There's only one way to start an outing in Grand Central, and that's by telling your date to meet by the clock. You'll follow in the footsteps of five generations of New York couples and travel companions by finding one another at the foot of the famous information booth, underneath the four-sided, opal-faced clock, valued by Sotheby's and Christie's at between $10 million and $20 million. The acorn that festoons the clock's top is a symbol of the family of Cornelius Vanderbilt, who built the original Grand Central depot and whose motto was "From the acorn grows the mighty oak." (Not to be outdone, the clock on the outside of the building, facing Park Avenue, holds the largest example of Tiffany glass on its face. Surrounding the clock is a sculpture called *Transportation*, which depicts Mercury, Hercules, and the goddess Minerva, Roman deities of speed, strength, and wisdom, respectively. Debate till your heart's content on the symbol of female brain alongside male brawn—or just leave it be and get on with the date.)

If you want to give your sweetheart red-carpet treatment, there's no better place to do it than Grand Central: it's thought that the term was coined here, to describe how the passengers of the luxurious 20th Century Limited (an express train that ran between New York and Chicago) embarked from a crimson-colored carpet spread over the platform. These days, however, that metaphorical pampering might take place at the **Oyster Bar** *(89 East 42nd Street, inside Grand Central Terminal, lower level; www. oysterbarny.com)*, the beautiful subterranean restaurant that specializes in bivalves and bubbly. But consider yourself warned: the vaulted tile ceilings create strange acoustics, and the sweet nothings you utter just might be heard across the bar! The auditory fun continues just outside the restaurant in what is known as the Whispering Gallery, where you can speak a soft message to your partner from across the room and have it delivered sonically via the arched ceiling. (For a visual primer on how to do this, check out the selection of Whispering Gallery marriage proposals on YouTube.)

One flight up and somewhat lesser-known is the site of the Kissing Room, also known as the Biltmore Room. This white marble chamber, set off from the main concourse, was where long-distance travelers would greet their families upon returning. During World War II, when it served as the reunification area for soldiers and their sweethearts, it became known as the Kissing Room, and authorities were known to turn a blind eye to couples flouting the city's official regulations on displays of affection.

After you've tired of exploring, retire to the **Campbell Apartment** *(15 Vanderbilt Avenue, between East 42nd and 43rd Streets; www.hospitalityholdings.com)* for a nightcap. Located in the former private offices of transportation tycoon John W. Campbell, this dimly lit cocktail lounge has been restored to show off its Jazz Age opulence after having spent several decades as a transit police closet. After your drink, duck into the terminal's Vanderbilt Hall just to see what's on. Exhibitions held in this space have included fashion shows, art exhibits, craft fairs, and product launches. Finish your evening with a kiss underneath the 2,500 stars of the zodiac-painted ceiling in the main concourse. *All locations are inside Grand Central Terminal, which is at East 42nd Street between Lexington and Vanderbilt Avenues, in Manhattan. www.grandcentralterminal. com. Subway: 4, 5, 6, 7, S to Grand Central–42nd Street.*

THE HOLIDAY DATE

Christmastime in New York offers a special brand of date-worthy itineraries, many featuring famed and iconic city landmarks and focused on seasonal events, spectacles, and festive decor. And since most of the highlights are outside, they invite you and your date to get close to keep warm as you take in the sights.

The first stop on your itinerary won't take place before twilight, leaving you free to stay cozy under the blankets in your hotel room until after many of the tourists have gone home. By touring Manhattan's department store Christmas windows in the evening, not only will you avoid the worst of the crowds, but the illumination of the tableaux behind the glass will also shine that much brighter. Start with **Barneys** *(660 Madison Avenue, between East 60th and 61st Streets; www.barneys.com)* to see the ever-amusing avant-garde creations of Simon Doonan; then shift over to Fifth Avenue to hit **Bergdorf Goodman** *(754 Fifth Avenue, between West 57th and 58th Streets; www.bergdorfgoodman.com),* **Henri Bendel** *(712 Fifth Avenue, between West 55th and 56th Streets; www.henribendel.com),* and **Saks Fifth Avenue** *(611 Fifth Avenue, between East 49th and 50th Streets; www.saksfifthavenue.com).* Across the street from Saks is the Rockefeller Center tree (its lights are on until 11:30 p.m. daily), as well as the ice rink, should you and your date be up for a nighttime skate. *(See page 28.)* If you're ready to warm up, head back up to 56th Street, where you'll find the midtown outpost of **Momofuku Milk Bar** *(15 West 56th Street, between Fifth and Sixth Avenues; www.milkbarstore.com).* There you can undo all the good of your walk with compost cookies and slices of crack pie. If you aren't too chilled, try the soft serve, which will undoubtedly be flavored for the season (past Yuletide flavors have included Stollen loaf, orange and clove, gingerbread, and sugar cookie). *Subway: N, Q, R to Fifth Avenue–59th Street.*

The Rockefeller tree is the city's most famous, but it certainly isn't the only tree in town at Christmastime. Inside the American Museum of Natural History, there is a special tree decorated with origami ornaments. The tree has a different theme every year (past themes have included "Discovery" and "The Biggest and the Best"), and volunteers begin folding the previous July to reach more than 500 ornaments come holiday time. If you are wandering around the east side, don't forget to look up and down Park Avenue, where there are trees and lights decorating each planted median on every block from East 47th to East 96th Streets.

You'd expect **the New York Botanical Garden** *(see page 117)* to have some trees come holiday time, but even more exciting is their annual holiday train show, in which New York City is reimagined in bark, mulch, and moss. In the show, visitors watch model trains travel across a Brooklyn Bridge made out of twigs and past a Lady Liberty wrapped in green grass. Nearly 150 city landmarks are created using botanical materials, with new ones added each year. (A recent addition was a working model of the Roosevelt Island tram.) The show runs from mid-November through early January, and advance tickets are strongly recommended.

This is the city that never sleeps, and many of our restaurants observe the holiday by keeping their doors open on Christmas Eve and Christmas Day—two days that are well-suited to a romantic meal à deux. For a proper Italian Feast of the Seven Fishes on Christmas Eve, try the **John Dory** in the Ace Hotel *(1196 Broadway, between West 28th and 29th Streets; www.thejohndory.com)*. On Christmas Day, feasts are offered at upscale gastronomic palaces such as **Bouley** *(163 Duane Street, between Hudson Street and West Broadway; www.davidbouley.com)* and **Nougatine** *(see page 92)*—as well as at pretty much every restaurant in Chinatown, the traditional destination of the city's most devout non-celebrators. (Calling in advance for reservations on either of these days is recommended—except for Chinatown—as some restaurants have set menus and special seatings.)

A STATUE BY ANY OTHER VIEW

The **Statue of Liberty** and the New York skyline are the two pinnacles of our visual signature, but the only way to catch a glimpse of this couple together is by boat. While the **Circle Line** *(www.circleline42.com)*, with its chuckle-inducing loudspeaker narration, is the traditional ride, **Manhattan by Sail's** petite fleet of two beautiful vessels make the former feel like a Greyhound bus. The pretty schooner the *Shearwater* is a romantic Gatsby-era yacht, hand-built with beautiful wood details. *Clipper City* is a tall ship, with masts that stretch 120 feet into the air, a replica of a nineteenth-century cargo schooner. While trips on both boats give breathtaking from-the-water views of the city skyline, the Statue of Liberty, and Ellis Island, the *Shearwater* is more intimate and better suited to a sail date, particularly if you select the sunset sail, which is timed so that passengers see the sun go down behind the Statue of Liberty. *Ninety-minute daytime sails start at around $45 per person; evening and sunset sails at about $50, which includes a complimentary cocktail.* Shearwater *sails depart at North Cove Marina in Battery Park;* Clipper City *sails depart from Pier 17 at the South Street Seaport. For more information, schedules, and to purchase tickets, visit www.manhattanbysail.com.*

THE BRUNCH DATE

Many New Yorkers call brunch their favorite meal of the week, so much so that although it was once the exclusive province of Sunday, it is now easy to come by on Saturday as well. Restaurants all over the city serve brunch, each putting their particular twist on the cherished meal. There are ramen brunches, bagel-and-lox brunches, curry brunches, pizza brunches—in addition to, of course, the traditional eggs, pancakes, and Bloody Marys. And if that weren't enough, in common parlance, the meal category has been unofficially extended to include restaurants that don't create a special brunch menu, so that across the five boroughs, the term "brunch" is loosely taken to mean any meal that happens between early morning and late afternoon on either weekend day.

Brunch followed by shopping, a movie, a museum trip, or a walk in the park is somewhat of a local institution, and for some, the selection of a brunch spot is determined as much by what it's close to as by what is served. The few places we've highlighted here offer a small cross section of the city's offerings and are places that, for different reasons, are well-suited for couples and can easily be integrated into a daylong activity with someone you love.

COOKSHOP. Certain neighborhoods in the city better suit certain moods. Chelsea, of course, means art—it's a good walking neighborhood, from the High Line to the sidewalk to the gallery floor, and therefore a dependable place to take someone you want to spend some quiet time with. On top of all there is to look at (and talk about), there's also no shortage of places to eat in Chelsea, one of the very best of which is Cookshop, the informal outpost of celebrity chef Marc Meyer. Brunch at Cookshop feels like a very social affair even when you're there for something as intimate as a date; it's a large, airy, beautiful space with walls of windows looking out at the High Line and the rush of Tenth Avenue, and it's simply always bustling during brunch hours on weekends. There's a long bar at which to wait for your table—arrive early, and get a head start on things with one of Cookshop's reassuringly strong Bloody Marys. The trick to making the most of Cookshop is to suppress the desire to experiment with the more adventurous (and sometimes risky) specials that decorate the menu and instead to stick with the classics. Cookshop's mildly Southern take on the humble joys of breakfast are among the finest in the city, from perfectly grilled bacon to delicate grits, light pancakes and pastries, and the mouthwatering (and sleep-inducing) Cookshop Scramble. We suggest you work up an appetite with a stroll up the High Line from the Meatpacking District, and walk the brunch off with a gentle turn around the galleries. *156 Tenth Avenue, between West 19th and 20th Streets, in Manhattan. 212-924-4440. www. cookshopny.com. Subway: C, E to 23rd Street; 1 to 18th Street or 23rd Street.*

DINER. The sister restaurant of the more serious Marlow & Sons next door, Diner is a lovely place for a brunch date because it strikes the perfect balance between high and low, fancy and informal. Housed in a nicely decrepit old diner car, and with a small garden outside for the warmer months, Diner manages to be intimate and busy, cozy and exciting all at the same time. It's always full on weekend mornings (or rather, afternoons) with an entertaining range of brunchers, from partied-out friends waking up late to young local couples reading the papers to overly dressed visiting Manhattan gourmands. Suitably for so eclectic a clientele, Diner's brunch menu is a cosmopolitan selection of consoling dishes, with a few familiar names (such as their reliably delicious and perfectly grilled burger) supported by a rotating cast of more adventurous specials. The latter can range from small but luxurious indulgences like their fruit scone, which is served in the English style with an unforgivably large portion of clotted Devonshire cream, to heartier fare for recovering from a hangover, such as grilled duck hearts. The waiters and waitresses still practice the charming discipline of scribbling the specials on your paper placemats as they describe them (and they're always worth remembering). There's something seductive about the rustic feel of the food, which contrasts nicely with the very urban location—try tucking into something as wholesome as bratwurst with tatsoi, runner beans, and a fried egg, or the country breakfast with biscuits and gravy, on a warm Brooklyn morning in the shadow of the Williamsburg Bridge. Follow it all with a stroll along the hipster's shopping mecca of Bedford Avenue, and you'll turn a standard New York weekend morning into a memorable and romantic day. (But maybe that's what brunch is all about?) *85 Broadway, between Wythe Avenue and Berry Street, in Brooklyn. 718-486-3077. www.dinernyc.com. Subway: J, M to Marcy Avenue.*

NOUGATINE. If you want to impress, whisk your date into Nougatine, the casual dining room in front of Jean-Georges, the three-Michelin-starred restaurant in the Trump Hotel Central Park. Even though it's been open for years, Nougatine is still considered by many New Yorkers to be a well-kept secret. The food is of the highest quality, if not as adventurous as the menus next door, and the service and atmosphere are befitting of a Michelin-starred operation. Yet there's never the crowd at Nougatine that one finds at many lesser restaurants around the city. On Sunday mornings, sunshine streams in from the floor-to-ceiling windows, offering glistening views of Columbus Circle and basking perfectly prepared French toast and eggs Benedict in a golden light. After your meal, you can pop across the street for a stroll in Central Park, or walk up six blocks to see what's on at Lincoln Center. *1 Central Park West, between West 60th and 61st Streets, in Manhattan. 212-299-3900. www.jean-georgesrestaurant.com. Subway: A, B, C, D, 1 to 59th Street–Columbus Circle.*

TELEPAN. The Upper West Side is a bastion for brunch, and for good reason: it's geographically positioned between two great parks (Central and Riverside), which are quintessential destinations for postprandial weekend strolls. The neighborhood was famously lacking in standout restaurants for many years, but its reputation as a gastronomic purgatory is largely outdated. One of the restaurants that did as much as any to elevate the neighborhood's culinary profile is Telepan, which has been open since 2005. It's wonderful at any time of day, but it's particularly lovely when you can bypass the more obvious, mediocre destinations along Columbus and Amsterdam Avenues and tuck into this hidden gem along a side street. Telepan's approach has changed little in concept since the restaurant opened in its devotion to seasonal ingredients, meticulous, beautiful presentation, and warm, pampering hospitality. After you've enjoyed a lobster and scallion omelet or a pancake soufflé topped with bacon (and polished off the simple macaroon cookie given to guests at the end of every meal), it's a short stroll to one of the aforementioned parks, a few blocks to Lincoln Center *(see pages 23, 61 and 81)*, or perhaps an opportune moment to familiarize yourself with more of our local, seasonal produce at the Sunday farmers' market in front of the American Museum of Natural History. *72 West 69th Street, between Central Park West and Columbus Avenue, in Manhattan. 212- 580-4300. www. telepan-ny.com. Subway: C to 72nd Street; 1, 2, 3 to 72nd Street.*

PRIME MEATS. The sibling of Frankies Spuntino *(see "Dinner and a Movie," page 79)*, Prime Meats is a local favorite for residents of Carroll Gardens and one of the area's destination restaurants, drawing people not just from the nearby Gowanus, Cobble Hill, and Red Hook neighborhoods, but also from as far afield as Manhattan. Famed for its cocktails and innovative bar staff, and with its focus on (you guessed it) a traditional carnivorous menu, Prime Meats combines a seductive old-world ambience with a considered masculine aesthetic, and its dark wood–paneled dining rooms are lit just brightly enough to see that your steak is cooked correctly. While it's lovely for lunch and dinner, it's at brunch that the restaurant feels its most inviting, with a bustling crowd and charming morning light warming the booths by the windows. The restaurant excels at classic brunch dishes and features a perfect burger, fluffy pancakes, and one of the finest eggs Benedicts in the city. On a warm day, there are tables outside facing an attractive corner of Court Street, but for the true romantic we suggest a cozy corner table inside, where a hearty brunch and a powerful cocktail or two can fortify and inspire a beautiful weekend. *465 Court Street, between 4th Place and Luquer Street, in Brooklyn. 718-254-0327. www.frankspm.com. Subway: F, G to Carroll Street or Smith–9th Streets.*

FREEMANS. Like many of Manhattan's most popular spots, Freemans is the subject of much debate among New Yorkers, who like to argue whether its considerable charms are worthy of enduring its considerable crowds. The answer, particularly when it comes to a couple looking for a romantic meal, is yes. Hidden at the end of Freemans Alley, between the trendiest downtown enclaves of NoLIta and the Lower East Side, Freemans is the epitome of the sexy brunch. A young and fashionable crowd restores their energies (after doubtless late nights) with cocktails from one of two bars while waiting for a table in one of the various equally cozy dining rooms. Among the first restaurants to define the hunting lodge aesthetic, Freemans has walls that are adorned with Arts and Crafts–style wallpaper and stylized taxidermy, creating the atmosphere of a chic upstate cabin. The menu, like the ambience, is at once traditional and decadent, with rich but simple dishes like skillet eggs with gruyere, the smoked trout plate, the Piedmontese cheeseburger, and their popular artichoke dip. There's always a line, so you'll probably have to wait for a table at any hour of the day—but couples nestling into one of the corner banquettes or taking a small table for two by the window can enjoy one of the most charming brunches downtown. *191 Christie Street, at the end of Freemans Alley, in Manhattan. 212-420-0012. www.freemansrestaurant.com. Subway: F to Second Avenue; J to Bowery.*

SARABETH'S. Almost as much a morning-meal institution as a bagel and shmear, the baked goods, outsize egg dishes, and world-famous jams at Sarabeth's are worthy grandes dames of the city's brunch scene. Sarabeth (yes, she is a real person and a real New Yorker, although she no longer produces all the jam she sells in her own kitchen) started feeding the city in 1981, when she opened a modest bakery near her home on the Upper West Side. In 1983—before many of the city's star chefs were even born—she opened this, her first restaurant, across the park. Since that time, the city has become a laboratory and testing ground for unconventional dining concepts and world-class gustatory inventions, and the enduring popularity of Sarabeth's proves that when you do something well, there's no need to reinvent the pancake (case in point: the lemon-ricotta variety that has been on the menus longer than we can remember). Homey and elegant, this original location (there are now five in Manhattan) is the one with the most heart, so make a point of coming here, and perhaps following your meal with a trip to the Cooper-Hewitt Museum or the Jewish Museum or a stroll in Central Park. *N.B.:* Brunch reservations are taken and strongly recommended. *1295 Madison Avenue, between East 92nd and 93rd Streets, in Manhattan. 212-410-7335. www.sarabethsrestaurants.com. Subway: 4, 5, 6 to 86th Street; 6 to 96th Street.*

PICNIC ITINERARIES

A picnic can be a wonderful way not only to do something fun and different that's a few buttons looser than a formal dinner date, but also a perfect excuse to explore the city's farther reaches—from its parks to its beaches, and from its greenmarkets to its purveyors of the perfect picnic fare. Needless to say, New York is a city of insistent seasons, at least one of which makes outdoor eating impossible (from November through March, give or take). All the more reason, then, for the true New Yorker to make the most of its glorious warmer months and the many beautiful parks and squares the city has to offer.

CENTRAL PARK. When local news stations give the weather forecast, they still quote the temperature in Central Park as the ultimate barometer. This is more romantic gesture than meteorological necessity—the park, as it is simply known (just as Manhattan is simply "the city"), remains New York's most beloved landmark, and it's the only instance of a tourist attraction being as valuable to locals as it is to visitors. It's also simply a beautiful park, which can continue to reveal mysteries and unveil secret spots even after you've lived in the city for years. Assuming your goal is to avoid the crowds and find a scenic spot to spread out on the grass, you can't really go wrong—no matter where you come into the park, follow the general rule that the farther in you are from the street, the more scenic and quiet it'll get. Our favorite suggestion is to enter the park on the Upper East Side—stopping at the Madison Avenue branch of **Dean & Deluca** (*1150 Madison Avenue, between East 85th and 86th Streets; www.deandeluca.com*) on the way, either for à la carte supplies or one of their brilliant seasonal picnic hampers—and make your way to the spot north of Conservatory Water, where you can feast in the company of Lewis Carroll's characters from *Alice in Wonderland*.

PROSPECT PARK—the pride of Brooklyn, Olmsted and Vaux's wilder gift to the city, and possibly the most beautiful green space in all the five boroughs—is unusual in that its many areas vary greatly in their landscape and mood. The formality of Grand Army Plaza bears no relation to the idyllic lake across the park at Windsor Terrace, and neither hints at the wilderness of the hilly Ravine or the seclusion of the carousel down by Ocean Avenue. The park also borders on several of the most dynamic and inviting neighborhoods in Brooklyn, and is therefore brilliantly positioned to provide picnickers with all manner of supplies for all manner of afternoons. One of our top recommendations is to stop by **Naidre's** (*384 Seventh Avenue, between 11th and 12th Streets, in Brooklyn; www.naidrescafebakery.com*), a cornerstone of Park Slope for more than a decade and a deli that strikes the perfect balance between conscience and indulgence. Here, you can pick up fresh sandwiches, fruit, salads, and an amazing selection of cakes (they're famous for their red velvet)—as well as great fair-trade coffee—and wander up to Prospect Park West, from where you can stroll down past the bandshell and find a tree to sit under on the Long Meadow. Romantics take note: the New York Philharmonic schedules free concerts in Prospect Park every summer, in which case an evening picnic would be a perfect date.

FORT GREENE PARK. With the Brooklyn Academy of Music a few blocks away and the Brooklyn Flea in its own backyard, Fort Greene has become one of the most popular places in the city for the young and the hip to eat, drink, live, date, and picnic. Although it's smaller by several acres than Prospect Park or even the botanic gardens, Fort Greene Park is one of Brooklyn's prettier and most eccentric green spaces, situated on an incline and with an unusually dynamic landscape that includes, of course, a fort. There are all kinds of options nearby for buying the ingredients of a great DIY picnic—**Smooch Organic** (*264 Carlton Avenue, between Willoughby and Dekalb Avenues, in Brooklyn; www.smoochorganic.com*), for their organic sandwiches and coffee, or the **Greene Grape** (*753 Fulton Street, between South Oxford Street and South Portland Avenue,* in Brooklyn; *www.greenegrape.com*) for their magnificent selection of cold cuts, breads, and cheeses. But the true aficionado will add a dash of spice to the alfresco date with a trip to the Brooklyn outpost of **Café Habana** (*757 Fulton Street, between South Oxford Street and South Portland Avenue, in Brooklyn; www.cafehabana.com*), an oasis of Cuban flavor and a highlight of the neighborhood in the warmer months. There, you can pick up fresh tacos and Mexican corn (grilled and served on the cob), and enjoy the delicious mess by the tower at the top of the hill in the park. And if you're extra sneaky, you can take your margaritas in to-go cups and pretend they're lemonades. . . . *Subway: G to Fulton Street; C to Lafayette Avenue.*

EMPIRE-FULTON FERRY STATE PARK AND BROOKLYN BRIDGE PARK. It is a truth universally acknowledged that looking *at* Manhattan is a lot nicer than looking *out* of it. With this in mind, the waterfronts of Brooklyn and Queens have in recent years been developed and redeveloped and redeveloped still, and some of the hot spots of the Brooklyn "riviera" are to be found at the freshly landscaped Empire–Fulton Ferry State Park and Brooklyn Bridge Park. The former is a beautiful triangle of green that sits between the Brooklyn and Manhattan Bridges, in the increasingly busy (and desirable) neighborhood of DUMBO, and aside from the bridges themselves boasts two of the city's most interesting structures, in the old tobacco factory behind the park and the pristinely restored carousel boxed jewel-like at its front. The latter extends south beyond the ferry terminal at the Brooklyn Bridge into the expanse of the water, offering wide-open views not only of the lower point of Manhattan but also of Governors Island and the busy waterways beyond. Pick up fresh fruit, salad, cold cuts, and breads from **Forager's Market** (*56 Adams Street, between Front and Water Streets, in Brooklyn; www.foragerscitygrocer.com*)—and maybe a box of delectable cookies and cakes from **One Girl Cookies** (*33 Main Street, between Water and Plymouth Streets, in Brooklyn; www.onegirlcookies.com*)—and stroll down the old cobbled streets and across the disused train tracks to the parks, and you'll enjoy an intensely urban view from an idyllic pastoral setting. *Subway: F to York Street; A, C to High Street.*

HUDSON RIVER PARK. Manhattan's premier waterfront park, the Hudson River Park, runs along the west side of the island, from West 59th Street all the way down through Battery Park City. Prime picnicking locations abound—benches facing the river, landscaped piers, and seemingly endless stretches of lawn—so if you and your mate find yourselves heading into the park on the spur of the moment, you really

can't go wrong. But if you are able to plan in advance, the south end of the park, below West 14th Street, feels more intimate than further up, where the lawns, piers, and verdant nooks are interrupted by Chelsea Piers, the *Intrepid*, and the Circle Line. Need provisions? **Chelsea Market** (*75 Ninth Avenue, between West 15th and 16th Streets, in Manhattan; www.chelseamarket.com*) is a good bet; you can create an ideal picnic smorgasbord with a loaf of bread from Amy's; antipasti from Buon Italia; a selection

The view of Manhattan from Brooklyn Bridge Park

of cheeses from Lucy's Whey; and for dessert, a Fat Witch brownie. From there, it's not such a long walk to the piers at Christopher and Charles Streets, where you can either spread a blanket on the (faux) grass, or set up on one of the extra-wide benches that encircle it. Public restrooms and water fountains are conveniently located right behind the piers, as is the Café at Pier 45, which has coffee, ice cream, and so-so food. If you are planning on settling further downtown, try making a quick run to the **TriBeCa Whole Foods** (*270 Greenwich Street, between Warren and Murray Streets; www. wholefoodsmarket.com*), picking up a bottle at **Chambers Street Wines** (*148 Chambers Street, between Greenwich Street and West Broadway; www.chambersstreetwines.com*), and having your date meet you at the corner of Chambers and West Streets. Right behind Stuyvesant High School is a lovely, rather secluded lawn, with a few trees for shade. No matter where in the park you land, you'll be treated to lovely views across the river, and if you time it right, you can watch the sun go down over New Jersey. *Hudson River Park runs along the west side of Manhattan from West 59th Street to Battery Park City. For more information, visit www.hudsonriverpark.org. Subway: A, C, E to 59th Street–Columbus Circle, 42nd Street–Port Authority Bus Terminal, 34th Street–Penn Station, or 14th Street; 1 to Houston Street or Canal Street; 2, 3 to Chambers Street.*

PERFECT PAIRINGS AND BEAUTIFUL COMPROMISES

New York is one of the dining capitals of the world, and one of the reasons for this is that we're a big fat melting pot made up not only of different nationalities, cultures, and races, but also of adventurous eaters, globe-trotting chefs, and devotees of every culinary movement and dietary regimen under the sun. Thus, it follows that the idiosyncratic side of the city's dining scene is made of restaurants that expertly and unexpectedly bring together different foods, themes, or styles on their menus and have them meet like in a screwball comedy. These tend to be small places a little under the radar, with owner-chefs still in the kitchen, obviously trying to realize their singular dream of togetherness in the big city—in short, the perfect places for a table for two.

CASELLULA. This tiny restaurant a little off the beaten path of the Theater District elevates wine and cheese to a new level. Cheese plates are the specialty of the house, and the staff can guide you through their selection of over forty domestic and international varieties and design a flight of cheeses (accompanied by wine or beer) tailored to your preferences. Each cheese is served with its own special condiment, which can range from traditional fruit paste and honey, to lavender popcorn, nut brittle, and house-made pickles and relishes. In addition, there is a full menu of cheese-focused salads, grilled sandwiches, and main dishes. The room is intimate yet bustling with energy, and the lighting is flatteringly dim. And while it is worth a trip in itself, if you and your date are headed to a Broadway show, you'll earn extra points by suggesting that you meet first to share a cheese plate at this little gem. *410 West 52nd Street, between Ninth and Tenth Avenues, in Manhattan. 212-247-8137. www.casellula. com. Subway: C, E to 50 Street.*

UPSTATE. Oysters are legendary aphrodisiacs; beer is maybe a less obvious choice to center a romantic meal around, but curious couples should seek out Upstate, a tiny East Village bar and restaurant that specializes in oysters and craft beer. Oysters arrive daily from the East and West Coasts, and the restaurant boasts not having a single freezer as proof of the freshness of each night's offerings. The beer menu also rotates regularly, though drafts are confined to New York state craft-beer producers (hence the restaurant's name). Upstate is run by a husband-and-wife team, a pairing which adds an extra layer of romantic charm on top of the reclaimed barn wood and timber that the bar is made from (also from upstate). So you are in the know, a homemade whiskey cake is served as a complimentary after-dinner treat. *95 First Avenue, between East 5th and 6th Streets, in Manhattan. 917-408-3395. www.upstatenyc.com. Subway: 6 to Astor Place; F to Second Avenue; L to First Avenue.*

FAT RADISH. The old nursery rhyme about Jack Sprat is like a metaphor for the modern condition: with so many special diets, it's the rare couple that can happily enjoy the same restaurant equally. Fat Radish is a scenester Lower East Side restaurant that offers mouthwatering meals for both sides of the table. For meat eaters, there's lamb, the signature Fat Radish burger with fries prepared in duck fat, and multiple nightly offerings of fresh seafood dishes. For the vegetarians, there are farmers' market plates, veggie pot pies, and entrées featuring seasonal vegetables. For those who care about it, there's a list of local farms and purveyors written on a mirror in the dining room; for those who don't, there's a cocktail menu to peruse and many beautiful people to watch. The restaurant serves nightly dinners, weekend brunch, and weekday lunch, so all you have to agree on is what time to visit. *17 Orchard Street, between Hester and Canal Streets, in Manhattan. 212-300-4053. www.thefatradishnyc.com. Subway: B, D to Grand Street; F to East Broadway.*

GRAPE AND GRAIN, AGAINST THE GRAIN. She likes her Syrah while he prefers a pilsner? Not a problem at these dual haunts deep in the East Village. As the names imply, these adjacent establishments specialize in wine and beer, so couples with opposing imbibing habits can coexist peacefully across the table. (At both establishments, you can order from either drink menu.) Grape and Grain is the charming, candlelit restaurant and the wine specialist—offering a European-focused wine selection in quarto and bottle sizes and an interesting menu of pizzas, salads, and other sharing plates. Next door is the more bar-style Against the Grain, where beer aficionados can geek out on the seventy-plus unusual selections, organized by color. Grape and Grain has the more intimate, traditionally date-like atmosphere, while Against the Grain has more of a tavern-style feel and a big communal table called the Mingler, which is where you'll go if you want to meet the regulars. *620 East 6th Street, between Avenues B and C, in Manhattan. 212-420-0002. www.grapeandgrain.net. Subway: F to Second Avenue; L to First Avenue.*

DATES TO TEASE YOUR GRAY MATTER

"Human beings are divided into mind and body. The mind embraces all the nobler aspirations, like poetry and philosophy, but the body has all the fun." So said Woody Allen, whose voice has come to epitomize the mixture of high and low we associate with the city herself, in *Love and Death*. New York is unusual in having as much to satisfy animal instincts as to satiate such higher aspirations. Home to some of the world's most prestigious literary festivals, the most celebrated art-house cinemas, legendary theaters and dramatic spaces, and hundreds of venues for readings, the city has something to raise even the highest brow a fraction higher. "My brain," Woody also said, "it's my second favorite organ." Even if we are polite enough to pretend Woody meant his heart to take the top spot, the point remains the same: that intellectual stimulation is as important as any other kind. So below are some suggestions for romantic distractions that embrace those nobler aspirations—at least as an entrée to the fun.

WHO KNEW LIBRARIES COULD BE THIS MUCH FUN?

The jewel in the city's literary crown is the New York Public Library building at Bryant Park, in midtown. More than a century old and one of the largest Beaux-Arts buildings in America, the central branch of the public library is a historic landmark. A fully functioning lending library and place of research and respite for scholars by

Fortitude, one of two lions that flank the steps of the New York Public Library (the other being Patience)

day, the library turns into one of the premier spots in town for literary and cultural events at night.

LIVE from the NYPL is a program of lively talks and panel discussions curated (and often led) by the series' director, the charismatic Paul Holdengraber. Events are advertised on the library's website many weeks in advance, so you can pick one that makes sense for the object of your affections. Subjects vary from readings by world-renowned authors to political debates, musical performances, and interviews between Holdengraber and a cultural icon or two. Crowds are passionate and always dotted with local literati, which makes events here fun, provocative, and exciting. It's the perfect mix of glamour and gray matter for a thoughtful date.

With one of the city's prettiest gardens on its doorstep, it'd be a crime not to suggest meeting first at **Bryant Park**. If it's a nice evening, stop by one of the kiosks near Sixth Avenue and have lemonade or an ice cream at one of the tables by the lawn. On a chillier night, meet for a hotter (or harder) drink at the bar of the **Bryant Park Grill** (*25 West 40th Street, between Fifth and Sixth Avenues, in Manhattan; www.arkrestaurants.com/bryant_park.html*), the ritzy restaurant that overlooks the park from a terrace backing onto the library itself. After the event you'll have plenty to talk about, so to continue the evening with a high brow and in a literary vein, walk a couple of blocks to the **Algonquin Hotel** (*59 West 44th Street, between Fifth and Sixth Avenues, in Manhattan; www.algonquinhotel.com*) and enjoy drinks and supper in the very room where Dorothy Parker held court at the round table. Alternatively, we'd suggest strolling out across the park to the **Cellar Bar** at the Bryant Park Hotel (*40 West 40th Street, between Fifth and Sixth Avenues, in Manhattan; www.cellarbarbryantpark-hotel.com*), a subterranean lounge where you can find a cozy corner and embrace noble aspirations over cocktails until the real fun starts.

MOVIES FOR SMART FOLKS

For those who hold cinema in high regard, lining up at a multiplex on a busy Friday night for a blockbuster and a $7 Coke isn't the best way to let the silver screen light up a romantic evening. If you or your loved one are the kinds of people who recognize the difference between going to the movies and seeing a film, then rejoice: New York is a city that discriminates, too, and caters better to high-minded cinephiles than any other city in America. There are a handful of small theaters well placed around the city that show a constantly changing but reliable mix of contemporary art-house films, edgy documentaries, and classics from the golden age to the new wave. Each comes with its own caveats—don't expect arena seating or nachos in a twelve-seat reel-to-reel projection room—but such details can nonchalantly be dismissed as evidence of charm. (*See also "Dinner and a Movie" at the beginning of this chapter for more of the city's treasured movie theaters and ways to make a date out of visiting them.*)

The **Albert Maysles Cinema** (*343 Lenox Avenue, between West 127th and 128th Streets, in Manhattan; www.maysles.org/mdc/*) is an enduring beacon of Harlem's culture, an art-house theater specializing in hard-hitting documentaries and profiles of international musicians. The only independent theater north of midtown, the Maysles is hidden inside a shabby old townhouse on Lenox Avenue and has a small auditorium that can be quiet and intimate one night and rowdy and fun the next. Proudly community-oriented, the Maysles screens productions by young local filmmakers and work by well-known directors—including films by the man the institute is named for. You won't find much in the way of snacks, but **Sylvia's** (*328 Malcolm X Boulevard, between West 126th and 127th Streets, in Manhattan; www.sylviasrestaurant.com*), one of Harlem's finest soul-food restaurants, is just down the street and the perfect place to chew over the movie afterward.

The **Anthology Film Archives** (*32 Second Avenue, between East 1st and 2nd Streets, in Manhattan; www.anthologyfilmarchives.org*) is at once a museum dedicated to the preservation of art-house cinema and a staple of the downtown movie theater circuit. The programs at the Anthology are curated with an eye toward new and emerging edgy American directorial talents, but they also run plenty of underground classics, from overlooked masterpieces of the 1960s and 1970s to hidden gems of the silent era. The atmosphere is a little rougher than most—the Ziegfeld this is not—but it draws a passionate crowd, and when you come out to the heart of the East Village, you'll have plenty of options for drinks afterward.

Film Forum (*209 West Houston Street, between Sixth Avenue and Varick Street, in Manhattan; www.filmforum.org*) is probably the best-known of the city's independent theaters. An icon of the pioneering cultural awareness of the West Village, Film Forum has been a nonprofit theater since 1970, dedicating itself fully to the continuation of a broad and thoughtful program. With a focus on international film and a fondness for the greats, the calendar here should be watched carefully because runs can be brutally short. Time your date right, and you could treat someone to a once-in-a-lifetime showing of a favorite old classic on the big screen. After the curtain comes down, we suggest you stroll up Seventh Avenue South to the hidden speakeasy **Little Branch** (*20 Seventh Avenue South, between Leroy and Clarkson Streets, in Manhattan; 212-929-4360*), where world-class bartenders in suspenders and moustaches can make you a bitter cocktail to sober you up after the flick.

HEY, DO YOU READ HERE MUCH?

Our city's literary history ranges from the glorious (E. B. White, the Algonquin Round Table), to the tragic (Dylan Thomas and Truman Capote, whose downfall came as a result of the publication of his tell-all novella about New York society, *La Côte Basque*). To attend a literary reading here allows anyone to tap into the mysterious romantic energy of the word. While the boroughs are full of prize-winning lions—not to mention countless numbers of lesser-known scribes toiling away on novels and memoirs—you don't have to be a writer to enjoy a literary event in this city. There are many venues across the five boroughs that offer exposure to prose and poetry in date-worthy settings.

For a date-oriented, theater-like evening, you'll want to head up to **Symphony Space** *(2537 Broadway, between West 94th and 95th Streets, in Manhattan; www.symphonyspace.org)* and secure a ticket for **Selected Shorts**. Started in 1985, these one-of-a-kind performances pair pieces of short fiction (new and classic) with distinguished stage actors. The show, which is broadcast nationally on public radio, was hosted by Symphony Space cofounder Isaiah Sheffer from 1985 until his death in 2012, and is now hosted by BD Wong, of *Law & Order* fame. From fall through spring, it attracts the best of the best from our great den of literary and thespian lions, including works by Raymond Carver, John Cheever, Flannery O'Connor, David Sedaris, and Haruki Murakami, read by Alec Baldwin, Cynthia Nixon, and Leonard Nimoy, among others.

In addition to being the home base for many writers, New York is also the center of the book-publishing industry, and if a writer with a new book is going to do an event in just one city, it usually happens here. Visiting bibliophiles should seek out their favorite literary authors in some of our beloved independent bookstores. A few to try are **McNally Jackson** in SoHo *(see page 45)*, **192 Books** in Chelsea *(see page 52)*, **Powerhouse Arena** in DUMBO *(37 Main Street, between Water and Front Streets, in Brooklyn; www.powerhousearena.com)*, and **BookCourt** *(163 Court Street, between Pacific and Dean Streets, in Brooklyn; www.bookcourt.com)* in Cobble Hill. All of these stores have multiple free readings and events per week, and you can find out what's coming up by visiting their websites or by picking up a current issue of *Time Out New York*, which lists upcoming literary events in their Books section.

If you see a shared *New Yorker* subscription as one of the biggest bonuses of cohabitation, you might want to plan a trip to the city in early October, when the New Yorker Festival takes place. For three days, you can see your favorite writers and *New Yorker* contributors speak in intimate settings all over the city. Friday events group different fiction writers under a theme (past events have included a discussion on utopia and dystopia with Margaret Atwood, Jennifer Egan, and George Saunders, and a conversation between novelists Jonathan Franzen and Jhumpa Lahiri). Other events during the three-day festival include museum visits and walking tours with staff writers and critics like Calvin Trillin and Peter Schjeldahl, film screenings, and conversations between *New Yorker* editors and figures in art, fashion, culture, and politics. The reliably beautiful weather and trees on the cusp of foliage season create the perfect setting for a pair of bookworms. *For upcoming festival dates, schedules, and ticket information, visit www.newyorker.com/festival.*

FINDING ROMANCE IN (THE CITY'S) UNEXPECTED PLACES

Anyone who's ever fallen in love knows you can't play it by the book. Love is never predictable, and until it happens, you never know whether your true love will be your college sweetheart or the doctor in the emergency room.

And so it is with the city. Finding the romance in New York needn't mean limiting yourself to landmarks and grand gestures, or hideaways and candlelight. Instead, once you know the five boroughs well enough, the city offers any number of activities that might seem on the surface to be mere quotidian distractions, but in fact—in the unique atmosphere of New York—afford all the romance of a gondolier's serenade.

Sit by the dog run in Tompkins Square Park

It may sound uninspired, but dog watching is something of a popular pursuit all over the city—as much for singles hoping their hound rubs noses with somebody's cute canine as for couples daydreaming about a future of lazy mornings and dog walks with their beloved. You can apply the same formula to any neighborhood with a cute and popular dog run, such as the West Village (Washington Square Park), the Upper East and West Sides (Central Park), and Park Slope (Prospect Park). Tompkins Square Park's run is the perfect place to stop after a casual Sunday brunch—don't forget to grab a coffee at Ninth Street Espresso.

Take your date to the diamond

In New York, sports belong to everyone, not just the die hards with season tickets and a wardrobe of souvenir jerseys. Because of its languorous pace, baseball is an easy game to come to as a novice (or as a fan with a novice companion), and even people who don't like baseball, per se, enjoy sitting out on the diamond on a sunny afternoon, talking over drinks and snacks while the boys in pinstripes try to knock one out of the park. Both Citi Field (where the Mets play) and Yankee Stadium have undergone recent, much-needed sprucings up of facilities and dining options—though be sure to review allegiances in advance, as no self-respecting Yankees fan can be expected to feign a happy afternoon at Citi Field. *Yankee Stadium is located at 1 East 161st Street, in the Bronx. newyork.yankees.mlb.com. Subway: B, D, 4 to 161st Street–Yankee Stadium. Citi Field: 123-01 Roosevelt Avenue, at 126th Street, in Queens. newyork.mets.mlb.com. Subway: 7 to Mets–Willits Point.*

Check out some art openings in Chelsea on a Thursday night

In the art-world week, Thursdays are (and have always been) the new Saturday. Many exhibitions open to the public on Thursday evenings with open-door receptions and extended hours (usually from 6:00 p.m. to 8:00 p.m.). The westernmost blocks of Chelsea close to the Hudson, which hold the city's densest concentration of galleries and artists' studios, come alive with throngs of well-dressed, cultured, attractive- and eccentric-looking artsy types from all over town. It's an interesting (and inexpensive) New York date, and a fun occasion for which to dress up a little. Just keep in mind that many galleries close in August, and spring and fall are prime times for art season. *Galleries are located in the West 20s, between Tenth and Eleventh Avenues in Manhattan. Subway: C, E to 23rd Street.*

Make time for tea

New York's brunch scene can be harried enough to put anyone in the mood for a different take on a midday meal *(though we do have some suggestions; see page 90).* A more low-key daytime option is tea, which, when done right in this city, can be an easy and sweet way to share a daytime meal with the one you love. In Manhattan, the mini-chain **Alice's Tea Cup** *(www.alicesteacup.com)* isn't sleepy—on weekends, it's best to go later, after the brunch crowd has eaten—nor is it pretentious or scene-y. During the week and on weekend afternoons, it's a cozy, casual spot to share an abundant high tea, with scones, cream, and finger sandwiches. Over in Williamsburg, the **Roebling Tea Room** *(143 Roebling Street, between Metropolitan Avenue and Hope Street, in Brooklyn. Entrance is on Metropolitan; www.roeblingtearoom.com)* doesn't serve high tea, but it does have an extensive selection of exotic blacks, greens, herbals, and matés, and the old-fashioned setting—metal casement windows, cozy worn leather armchairs, and demure floral wallpaper—recalls an expat

MAKE-OUT SPOTS

Paris has the Seine. Hollywood has the hills and the drive-ins. And New York . . . well, New York does not have quite the Riviera of its old-world rivals or the vistas of its hillier counterparts. But there are parts of New York that make for destinations in and of themselves, even separate from all the restaurants and watering holes and cultural epicenters the city has to offer. They might be more like oases in an urban desert or even mirages visible only to those thirsty enough to see magic where others don't. But they're there—and nothing impresses a fellow romantic like a romantic who's romantic enough to find them.

Any New Yorker worth his or her salt should keep note of the kinds of spots they'd like to come back to another time with someone at their side, so our real advice here is to keep your eyes open. But if you need a little help, here are a few suggestions of places it's worth going to just to smooch:

- at the clock in the main hall at Grand Central;
- Woody Allen's and Diane Keaton's bench at Sutton Place;
- under the trees in the circular park at the northern end of the Brooklyn Promenade;
- in a rowboat on the lake at Central Park;
- in the photo booth at the Ace Hotel;
- in a pair of reclining seats at the AMC 84th Street movie theater;
- on the roof of the Met;
- in the private curtained booth at the Cha-An tearoom in the East Village;
- on a bench on the boardwalk at Coney Island;
- on adjoining sliding chairs at the High Line facing out over the Hudson.

hangout out of a Hemingway novel. For a more clandestine experience, try **Cha-An** (*230 East 9th Street, second floor, between Second and Third Avenues; www.chaanteahouse. com*), a small, hushed Japanese tearoom in the East Village's Little Tokyo, where you can choose from hundreds of teas and have well-trained waitresses pour from elegant teapots at your table. (You can even reserve the curtained-off booth for a little teatime privacy. . . .) **N.B.:** The Plaza, the Carlyle, and the Pierre Hotels all serve high tea as well, but the prices are steep, and the magic of discovery isn't the same as what you will find at these other locales.

OH (YES!), THIS OLD PLACE?

In New York, there are the classics (the Empire State Building, the Met), and then there are the stalwarts: the wonderful, reliable, tried-and-true-and-terrific restaurants that live through the first blush of opening buzz. In a city that offers up endless restaurant debuts and goes through food trends at a ravenous pace, it's all the more delightful to experience a meal at one of those places that has survived the fickle heart of this city's dining scene (whether for centuries or merely decades). Given the rapid pace of development that has rid the city of a number of beloved establishments (RIP Florent, and the original Café des Artistes), restaurants, such as the following, that remain appealing and worth visiting after many years are becoming an increasingly rare breed.

THE 21 CLUB. The phrase "If these walls could talk" could have been invented to describe the scene at the 21 Club, the historic Prohibition-era speakeasy that has survived police raids, concealed crates and crates of liquor in underground passageways, and seen an untold number of romantic liaisons, illicit and otherwise. In fiction, it's where Fred spots Holly Golightly with one of her gentleman friends, and where the love triangle of Katy, Eve, and Tinker down martinis and oysters in style before a fateful return home in the novel *The Rules of Civility*. In reality, the 21 Club was the site of Bogey and Bacall's first date, and where JFK dined on the night of his inauguration. The most romantic spot is Upstairs at 21, the intimate dining room over the main bar area where only a prix-fixe menu is served. The dining room walls are painted with four murals depicting the city in the 1930s, the club's heyday. *Reservations recommended. Men must wear a jacket, although no tie is required. No jeans or sneakers allowed. 21 West 52nd Street, between Fifth and Sixth Avenues, in Manhattan. 212-582-7200. www.21club. com. Subway: E, M to Fifth Avenue–53rd Street.*

The entrance to the 21 Club

JOHN'S OF 12TH STREET. From the candelabra made from wine bottles concealed under cascades of dripping wax to the blood-red leather banquettes, every inch of this 107-year-old Italian restaurant is soaked in Prohibition-era lore. During the reign of the Volstead Act, John's was a notorious speakeasy; wine and whiskey were made in the cellar, and liquor was served in demure espresso cups. Where illicit liquor goes, the mob follows, and John's was, during this time, also a regular hangout of gangsters such as Arnold Rothstein and Lucky Luciano—a history that has been reenacted on the small screen in HBO's *Boardwalk Empire*, with John's playing itself. (The restaurant was later used in another episode in the series, this time playing a pharmacy called Whitings.) Even if you don't find the camaraderie of gangsters especially romantic, it's hard not to be taken in by John's authentic old-timey ambience, especially these days, when so many new restaurants try to claim history with naked lightbulbs and distressed wood. The centerpiece of this is the aforementioned candelabra, an homage to the restaurant's roots as a speakeasy featuring old wine bottles almost entirely concealed by intricate patterns of wax that have been dripping since Prohibition was repealed in the early '30s. (The wax is regularly pruned by the staff.) After being owned by friends of the original John's family since the 1970s, the restaurant was recently purchased by a partner of the trendy Beatrice Inn, as part of an amicable deal in which the new owner (and John's regular) pledges to preserve, rather than refurbish, this classic. *302 East 12th Street, between First and Second Avenues, in Manhattan. 212-475-9531. www.johnsof12thstreet.com. Subway: 6 to Astor Place; L to First Avenue or Third Avenue.*

ONE IF BY LAND, TWO IF BY SEA. The history of the city as we know it started in earnest during the Revolutionary War, when New York was captured by the British, and the city was an ongoing battlefield until the war ended in 1783. The carriage house at 17 Barrow Street was built in 1767 as part of an adjoining mansion belonging to an English dignitary. After the war, the mansion and carriage house were taken by George Washington and later purchased by Aaron Burr, then the state's Attorney General, who resided there until his death-by-duel in 1836. In the years following, the property belonged to famous millionaire John Jacob Astor, and then became a brothel, and finally an early silent-movie house. Tucked away on a picture-perfect West Village street, One If By Land, Two If By Sea has long been considered one of the city's (and the country's) most romantic restaurants, although for many years, the food was deemed not up to par. But a recently installed chef has brought the once-stuffy menu into the modern world with indulgent interpretations of old-timey classics, such as rabbit and beef Wellington. If the $125 tasting menu or $78 prix-fixe menu seems too rich for your blood, slink with your sweet over to the bar, where you two will be serenaded by live piano music over cocktails and hors d'oeuvres. *Reservations recommended. 17 Barrow Street, between West 4th Street and Seventh Avenue South, in Manhattan. 212-255-8649. www.oneifbyland.com. Subway: 1 to Christopher Street– Sheridan Square; A, B, C, D, E, F, M to West 4th Street.*

CHAPTER 4

FURTHER AFIELD

There is only one borough of New York that is connected to the contiguous forty-eight states (that would be the Bronx), and once you are inside the city, the comic geography of Saul Steinberg's iconic *New Yorker* cover—in which the world beyond bustling Tenth Avenue is represented by bland squares and blobs representing New Jersey, Kansas City, the Pacific Ocean, and China—can really take hold. The prevailing perspective is such that Manhattan can seem as outsized as a country, and the small river separating the boroughs from the rest of New York state, New Jersey, and all points west as metaphorically large as an ocean. So if you can find time in between visits to the museums along Fifth Avenue, strolls in Central Park, and shopping in SoHo—and we strongly advise that you do—it's deceptively easy and surprisingly rewarding to travel even slightly off the concrete-laden path. Variety is, after all, a potent spice.

The excursions in this chapter range from simple trips to places where you may still glimpse the city skyline in the background to lesser-known attractions within the city limits to nearby excursions to beaches, sculpture parks, and small towns. We start with some low-profile museums that live in neighborhoods that aren't the Upper East Side, then travel through the city's botanical gardens to neighborhoods and destinations at the tips of Manhattan, Queens, and Brooklyn, and hop over to some local islands. We end with excursions to the Hudson Valley, Westchester County, nearby Connecticut, and the east end of Long Island, a category of trips that are especially nice to consider if you can make an overnight of them. (While a car is not technically required to visit any of the places listed in this chapter, we've noted where one might be useful for a fuller visit of the area or more flexibility in schedule.)

First-time visitors to New York can be understandably reluctant to consider devoting a full afternoon or an entire day to a single, comparatively far-off attraction. After all, one of the beautiful things about the city is how much is packed into one relatively compact area, and how quickly one can get from place to place, thanks to our remarkable public transportation system. But particularly for those who have a long relationship with the city, who have come to know specific corners of museums, or who have a favorite table in a favorite restaurant, adding some new destinations to your repertoire can add an exciting layer to a pleasant but tried-and-true routine. Each of our suggestions will remind you of this city's lovely paradox: it's because of how much has been crammed into a relatively small bit of land—and not in spite of it—that you can take a short journey and be somewhere that feels completely removed.

BEYOND MUSEUM MILE

It says a lot about the cultural largesse of this city that you could take away the Met, MoMa, the Whitney, the Guggenheim, and the rest of Museum Mile and still be left with more than enough museums for a vacation's worth of visitations. These venerable stalwarts live up to their world-class reputations, no doubt, but they also tend to obscure more modest gems in neighborhoods far from the well-traveled Fifth Avenue corridor. The beauty of Museum Mile is, of course, convenience and centrality. When looked at another way, a museum that requires a dedicated journey takes away the pressure to create a hectic itinerary, minimizes the risk of overstimulation, and allows you to experience a pocket of this grand city that you might otherwise have overlooked: Long Island City and its riverfront Manhattan views; Washington Heights, where the island of Manhattan narrows; and the Riverdale section of the Bronx, overlooking the Hudson River and the Palisades.

NOGUCHI MUSEUM. Hidden behind the high walls of an old industrial building in the Queens neighborhood of Long Island City, the Noguchi Museum is one of the most charming and peaceful places in all of New York. Unlike the noisy hordes at the MoMA or the shuffling crowds in the galleries of the Met, the relative few who make the effort to find it are rewarded with as sensual an experience as any museum can offer. Designed by the enigmatic and influential Japanese-American artist Isamu Noguchi to house his work, the museum is an oasis of cool concrete, stone, glass, and light. While its collection includes works in many media—from drawings on paper and portraits in clay to experiments in urban planning—the real reason to visit is the sculpture garden outside the galleries. Beneath cherry trees and weeping willows, Noguchi's smooth sculptures hide among Japanese greenery while a fountain quietly wets the pebbles of the path around the garden. Sheltered from the sounds of the city, the garden is that rare thing: a public space that feels like it's yours, intimate even with strangers alongside you. Sit on a bench here and hold hands after a stroll around the galleries, and it'll feel like the artist created the garden just for you. *9-01 33rd Road, between 9th and 10th Streets, in Queens. 718-204-7088. www.noguchi.org. Subway: N, Q to Broadway.*

MORRIS-JUMEL MANSION. This mansion museum in Washington Heights is the oldest house in Manhattan, and as such, its walls have witnessed plenty over the past three centuries worth gossiping about. The mansion was built by a British loyalist couple just before the American Revolution in the romantic Palladian style (think porticoes and arched windows), and then after the couple's abrupt return across the pond it became the temporary headquarters of General George Washington. Through the turn of the nineteenth century, its salons and dining rooms hosted a bevy of Revolutionary-era luminaries (John Adams, Thomas Jefferson, and Alexander Hamilton were all dinner guests). The mansion's most colorful character, however, was the late proprietress Eliza Jumel. Jumel was the striving daughter of a New England prostitute, and she married Stephen Jumel, a wealthy French wine merchant, in 1804. The couple purchased the mansion in 1810, but they were spurned by New York society because of Eliza's low birth and traveled to France not long afterward, where Eliza became a supporter of Napoleon Bonaparte. This led to her forced return to New York and to the mansion without her husband. Here, she astutely managed their finances until Stephen's death in 1832. A year later, Eliza married the irascible politician Aaron Burr in the mansion's front parlor, and his squandering of her hard-won fortune led to their separation a few months later. (Their divorce was finalized on September 14, 1836, the day of Burr's death.) More recently, the mansion and its grounds have been a respite for sophisticated New Yorkers like Jacqueline Kennedy Onassis (who hosted luncheons and teas in the mansion's drawing rooms) and Katharine Hepburn. As a museum, the mansion is a far cry from the Met, but it's an impressive, venerable piece of architecture in our relatively young city, with grounds and gardens that are lovely to relax in. Special exhibitions offer surprisingly titillating takes on the mansion's history, with titles such as "Women Unbound" and "The Loves of Aaron Burr: Portraits in Corsetry and Binding." *65 Jumel Terrace, between West 160th and 162nd Streets, in Manhattan. 212-923-8008. www.morrisjumel.org. Subway: C to 163rd Street–Amsterdam Avenue.*

WAVE HILL. A little-known treasure of the pretty Riverdale section of the Bronx, not far north of the Harlem River that divides Manhattan from the mainland, Wave Hill succeeds in being many things at once. First and foremost, Wave Hill is a house, a beautiful old estate that has been the home at one point or another for such celebrated New Yorkers as Theodore Roosevelt and Mark Twain. In addition to the house, the Wave Hill estate occupies twenty-eight acres of some of the most gorgeous gardens in the five boroughs, ranging from lightly landscaped woods that feel as wild as the country across the Hudson to formal European flower gardens and conservatories. But Wave Hill is more than just a house and garden; its stated mission is to improve New Yorkers' relationships with the natural world "through programs in horticulture, education, and the arts." Whether or not you have time to check out their schedule of classes, exhibitions, and other special events, a trip to Wave Hill can be enlightening in all kinds of ways. The real joy of the place is its position high on the rocky edge of the city, which in a beautiful natural setting affords the kinds of views for which romantics scale the skyscrapers of midtown. And hidden among the gardens, wherever the landscapes open up to views across the river or down toward Manhattan, are teak benches and pairs of deck chairs perfect for couples seeking only each other's company in the peace and quiet. *675 West 252nd Street, between Sycamore and Independence Avenues, in the Bronx. 718-549-3200. www.wavehill.org. Subway: 1 to Van Cortlandt Park–242nd Street (where the free Wave Hill shuttle bus will pick visitors up and drive them to the gardens; check website for times and details).*

BOTANIC GARDENS

New York, as many a resident likes to point out, is not really the concrete jungle it's made out to be. There are more than 600 community gardens across the five boroughs, in addition to 1,700 parks and playgrounds. The grandest of these are the city's botanical gardens, which offer a full, more formal way to have a bucolic retreat in the big metropolis. All of these gardens are popular sites for proposals and weddings (the Bronx and Brooklyn ones in particular must be booked at least a year in advance).

NEW YORK BOTANICAL GARDEN. Without taking anything away from its cousins around the city, the New York Botanical Garden in the Bronx is without a doubt the most beautiful green space in the five boroughs. More than 120 years old and designated a National Historic Landmark, the NYBG is a New York institution on par with the Met or Central Park. Situated in the heart of the Bronx, it's far enough from the busier parts of Brooklyn and Manhattan that many visitors to the city (not to mention many longtime residents who don't look far enough afield) won't make the trip. But it only takes twenty-five minutes from Grand Central Terminal to the park's own Metro-North station, and it makes for an enchanting and memorable day trip unlike any other. Conceived at the end of the nineteenth century, when the original Carnegies and Morgans and Vanderbilts of the city were still investing heavily in making New York's mark on the world, the NYBG was created with the lofty intention of being the most beautiful garden of its kind in the country, and a botanical institution to rival its long-standing European counterparts. Spread out over 250 acres, the garden is big enough that a couple can enjoy the sense of solitude afforded on a country walk as well as the refined sensibility of a manicured garden. Get lost in woodlands with centuries-old trees, and paddle in the Bronx River; or sit close on a bench out of sight in the herb garden, where every breeze brings different scents from the plants around you. Stroll along the mazelike paths of the perennial garden, where the palettes of the flowers are carefully designed to remain as vivacious and seductive as possible in every season; or spend an hour idling around the geometric lanes in the magnificent rose garden, which feels like a lost annex of the Jardin du Luxembourg, in Paris. At the heart of it all is the gorgeous Victorian-style Enid A. Haupt Conservatory, an enormous glasshouse in which special exhibitions alternate, each one prettier than the last. Wherever you walk in the garden, the abundant beauty of flowers and trees greets you at every turn. Whether you're simply looking for a lovely day out of the city or there's an important conversation to be had that requires the peace and privacy of such beautiful surroundings, the New York Botanical Garden is the place. *2900 Southern Boulevard, in the Bronx. 718-817-8700. www.nybg.org. Transportation: Metro-North Railroad Harlem Line to Botanical Garden.*

BROOKLYN BOTANIC GARDEN. While Brooklyn has no shortage of greenery these days—from the expanding Brooklyn Bridge Park to Fort Greene, McCarren, and Prospect Parks—nothing comes close to the borough's botanical garden for sheer beauty. Now a little more than a century old, the garden, which is found at the eastern side of Prospect Park between Flatbush and Washington Avenues, is so beautifully curated and carefully tended that it feels magical. Created over time, section by section, with individual botanists and landscapers shaping different parts of the park, it is also the most diverse botanical garden in the city, geared to change in keeping with the seasons, and a wonderful place to come for something as simple as a romantic stroll. Walking around the lake in the Japanese Hill-and-Pond Garden is transporting, with nothing but the sounds of the birds and ripples in the water from the koi that give the pond flashes of color. In spring, the trees in the Cherry Esplanade erupt into blossoms of whites and reds and pinks, and petals seem to escape to all corners of the park. In late April, Bluebell Wood bursts into bloom and makes a whole area of

The Museum Building and the Fountain of Life at the New York Botanical Garden

the park's woodland look as though it's carpeted in a beautiful lilac fabric. Small gardens like the Rock Garden and the Herb Garden are hidden along the way, and they are perfect places to pause and sit in relative secrecy for a while. And the Cranford Rose Garden—when visited at just the right moment—is one of the prettiest and most delicious-smelling places in the city. Our advice, for visitors to the city and for those fortunate enough to be able to devote a workday to it, is to avoid the crowds of the weekend and come early on a weekday, when there are few enough people to make you feel like the gardens belong to you alone. Picnicking is sadly forbidden, but there's no law against napping in shade in the prettiest corner you can find. *150 Eastern Parkway, between Underhill and Washington Avenues, in Brooklyn. 718-623-7200. www.bbg.org. Subway: 2, 3 to Eastern Parkway–Brooklyn Museum.*

SNUG HARBOR BOTANICAL GARDEN. The third and most secret of the city's botanical gardens is located on Staten Island, at the Snug Harbor Cultural Center. Snug Harbor is located on the north shore of the island, facing New Jersey, and is a short bus ride from the ferry terminal. If it's an intimate escape you are looking for—or surprising, inspiring, bucolic scenery—it's well worth the multipronged journey from Manhattan to the city's most independent borough. The centerpiece is the Chinese Scholar's Garden, one of only two authentic Chinese Scholar's Gardens in the country. Designed and developed in China before being constructed here in 1999, this elegant garden is based on the Couple's Retreat Garden, one of a number of classical gardens in the Suzhou region of China from the Qing Dynasty. The garden's name comes from its atypical design (which divides the space into east and west quadrants), but it's also the perfect moniker for a space of lush but quiet elegance. Elsewhere, there is the recently opened Tuscan Garden, modeled after Villa Gamberaia in Florence, Italy, which features beautifully landscaped terraces and formal water elements, as well as the Connie Gretz Secret Garden, a European-style children's garden and maze that was created by a Staten Island resident in loving memory of his young wife, who died of cancer at age 46. There are also rose gardens, shade gardens, and butterfly gardens scattered about the grounds, which were originally the site of a home for retired sailors. The utter picturesqueness of the wide variety of settings makes this a wonderful location for engagement photos, as well as an idyllic spot for a proposal. It's also a lovely location for weddings, indoors or out. *1000 Richmond Terrace, between Snug Harbor Road and Tysen Street, in Staten Island. 718-448-2500. www.snug-harbor.org. Transportation: If traveling by ferry from Manhattan, take the S40 bus at Gate D in the ferry terminal to Snug Harbor Cultural Center.*

ISLANDS AND OTHER FAR-FLUNG CORNERS

Once you're here, your horizon is limited by the impressive towers and the brownstones of the city's streets, and it's easy to forget that geographically—as in so many other ways—New York City is unique. It's a coastal city at the mouth of a great river, surrounded by waters that have created the rivers, bays, beaches, and palisades that define the varied landscape of the five boroughs. Just as New York has much to offer the romantic visitor in the way of culture, the city also provides an incredibly varied and seductive natural setting for all manner of romantic adventures. And the key to discovering the city's surprises is simply to explore.

Even the lifelong New Yorker still finds a thrill in crossing one of the city's many bridges—seeing the city's lights reflected in the water of the river as you drive (or ride a cable car!) from one borough to the next is something that never loses its power to take your breath away. But people—distracted, perhaps, by the joyful recognition that New York is really one united entity, a force greater than the sum of its parts—come to overlook the fact that the city is literally a collection of islands and landmasses joined together with bridges, tunnels, ferries, and waterways. The longer you have to spend in the city, the more reason you have to look beyond the obvious—the classic promenades, the beloved date spots, and the epicenters of the city's romantic cultural heritage—and find romance in the unexpected, in the far-flung corners and mysterious islands of the city.

Couples can visit New York dozens of times, for example, without ever knowing that at the very northern tip of Manhattan, hidden in the woodland of a beautiful landscaped park, a medieval European castle sits atop a rocky hill. Or that at the southwestern edge of Brooklyn, there's a neighborhood so wonderfully distinct from the rest of the city that it feels like a seaside town you might find on a drive up the coast. Or, perhaps most surprisingly of all, that some of the islands floating around Manhattan can offer sights, senses, and experiences that are every bit as romantic as the star attractions of Manhattan—which, lest we forget, is still an island after all.

THE CLOISTERS

Strictly speaking, the Cloisters is a museum, an outpost of the Metropolitan Museum of Art thát houses much of the Met's collection of medieval art. But before you even get to the admissions desk, a trip to the Cloisters is unlike a visit to any other museum in the world. The adventure begins when you get off the A train at

190th Street, far up the west side of Manhattan, where you find yourself on the cusp of Fort Tryon Park. One of the city's lesser-known parks, Fort Tryon was designed by Frederick Law Olmsted Jr., and so has some claim to New York landscaping heritage. Positioned on an incline high above the Hudson, facing the dramatic facades of the Palisades across the river, Fort Tryon is something of an uptown secret: a popular park for locals of Washington Heights and Inwood, it's also unusually well designed, with gently curving paths that take advantage of the steps and layers inherent in Manhattan's rocky landscape to offer stunning views of the river. The Cloisters museum—which comprises medieval buildings literally bought and brought over, stone by stone, from Europe—is situated on top of the hill at the

northern end of the park. The museum itself is rather small, intimate, and quaint, with the feeling of an ancient European castle perched at the tip of Manhattan. The collection is charming even if neither you nor your loved one are experts on medieval art and culture, and it includes objects—such as the beautiful unicorn tapestries—that must be kept sheltered in cool and dim light, which makes for a hushed and secretive atmosphere. After a stroll around the collection, there's a courtyard café where you can sip a cool drink and peer out through old stone windows across the treetops of the park below. The whole experience is slightly surreal and lends the northwest corner of Manhattan a mysterious and romantic aura that only very regular visits can do something to dispel. No matter how many times you visit, though, you may find the walk up the hill through Fort Tryon Park as perfect a corner of the city as any. *99 Margaret Corbin Drive, in Manhattan. 212-923-3700. www. metmuseum.org. Subway: A to 190th Street.*

RED HOOK

Perched on the edge of Brooklyn, in what one might think of as the "far west" of the borough, is the neighborhood of Red Hook. The term *oasis* is often used to describe peaceful pockets in the middle of the city; Red Hook is less a convenient respite than an escape to a different world. Geographically isolated, surrounded by water, and separated from the rest of Brooklyn by the Brooklyn–Queens Expressway (known to locals as the BQE), Red Hook feels more like a remote seaside town than a neighborhood in the most bustling metropolis in the world. It would be shortsighted to put a completely romantic spin on it—this neighborhood, like many in the city, was long plagued by crime and drugs—and today's charm is more gritty than glamorous. Nevertheless, like an irresistible rogue who bucks convention, Red Hook boasts individuality and idiosyncrasy in its many independent businesses (it's the home of New York City's only wine-making co-op and a waterfront business that sells nothing but Key lime pie), shows its romantic side in restaurants and cafés owned by couples living their dreams, and is the only neighborhood in the entire city where you can get a full-frontal view of Lady Liberty.

This is a waterfront town, with all of the history and trappings that entails. Its legacy as a tough shipping center was depicted in both the classic Marlon Brando film *On the Waterfront* and Arthur Miller's tragic romance, *A View from the Bridge.* Both Miller and Elia Kazan, who directed *On the Waterfront*, were inspired by the danger and roughness of that environment, and though it's been many decades since Red Hook served as an important port (before containerization, it was the busiest freight port in the world), this legacy still is visible in the docks and ship-yards that continue to function today. (The ocean liner *Queen Mary 2* docks at Red Hook's Brooklyn Cruise Terminal.)

For many New Yorkers, Red Hook is a destination they discover only when they visit IKEA, the Swedish furniture retailer that proudly set up its first shop within the city limits here, in 2008. (Along with Fairway supermarket, these are the only two mega-stores in an area otherwise known for its one-off, destination gems.) But visitors not in need of a Billy bookshelf should know that Red Hook—with its shops and restaurants and cobblestone streets and water views—is a destination in itself. Thanks to IKEA, there is a ferry that runs between Red Hook and lower Manhattan, which is free on weekends and $5 on weekdays (or free with a receipt from IKEA of $10 or more). From the ferry terminal, walk two blocks north to Van Brunt Street, which is the neighborhood's main drag, and begin your exploration. If you arrive first thing in the morning, start your day with a coffee and a pastry at **Baked** (*359 Van Brunt Street, between Wolcott and Dikeman Streets; www.bakednyc.com*), a beloved neighborhood bakery. Or if you need more of a meal, visit **Fort Defiance** (*365 Van Brunt Street, between Dikeman and Coffey Streets; www.fortdefiancebrooklyn.com*), an all-day joint named for a Revolutionary-era fort that was constructed during the Battle of Brooklyn. Both of these businesses are locally owned, and if you ask the proprietors for their particular local gems, you may well come up with a personalized itinerary filled with recom-mendations for the businesses owned by their friends and neighbors. Someone will likely point you in the direction of **Steve's Authentic Key Lime Pies** (*185 Van Dyke Street, at Ferris Street; www.stevesauthentic.com*), a perfect example of the neighbor-hood's one-of-a-kind treasures. This bakery looks straight out of Florida, but Steve has been in the neighborhood since the late 1990s. (After 2012's Hurricane Sandy, he moved his operation to the current location from the pier next door.) Steve makes pies in small batches using only five ingredients, and if you don't care for citrus, this probably isn't the place for you. But if tart is your thing, you'll find no better, fresher example. At the retail counter, your choices are ten-inch, eight-inch, and four-inch pies, or the Swingle, a four-inch pie dipped in chocolate and served on a stick. Another unique local business worth visiting is the **Red Hook Winery** (*175–204 Van Dyke Street, at Pier 41; www.redhookwinery.com*), an original operation in which two experienced winemakers split grapes from leased plots in the Finger Lakes and on the North Fork, and each creates distinct vintages. As you'll find in Napa Valley or the North Fork, there is a tasting room for visitors to sample these unusual, small-batch creations. Another local attraction is the **Waterfront Museum** (*290 Conover Street, at*

Pier 44; www.waterfrontmuseum.org), which is housed on a 1914 barge, and which, in addition to being a perfect showcase of maritime history, is also a very cool place to have a wedding. **N.B.:** This small museum has very limited opening hours, so be sure to check the website before planning a visit.

No day in Red Hook would be complete without a stop at the **Good Fork** (*391 Van Brunt Street, between Coffey and Van Dyke Streets; www.goodfork.com*), a strong candidate for most romantic restaurant in the entire city. There are cozy booths perfectly sized for couples inside an interior reminiscent of a ship's cabin, built by one of the owners (the other owner, his spouse, is the chef; she cooks with a delightful mix of Korean and American influences that, like the best marriages, complement each other in differences). If there happens to be a wait for a table when you arrive, they'll likely send you down the street to Fort Defiance for a cocktail (the owner used to be a tenant in their building). That's Red Hook—a small town on the edge of one of the biggest cities in the world. *The ferry to Red Hook leaves from Pier 11 in Manhattan, at Wall Street and the East River. For more information and schedules, visit www.nywatertaxi.com/tours/ikea.* **N.B.:** The closest subway stop to Red Hook is the F and G at Smith–9th Streets, which is about a half-hour walk away from IKEA and the waterfront. A more direct option is the B61 bus, which can be picked up in downtown Brooklyn. Visit www.mta.info for more information on bus stops. IKEA also runs a free shuttle bus during peak shopping hours from several Brooklyn subway stations. For more information on the shuttle stops and schedule, visit info.ikea-usa.com/Brooklyn/StoreDirections.aspx.

THE ROCKAWAYS

The Rockaways have been a beach resort for New Yorkers for almost 200 years, since entrepreneurs began building houses and hotels here for summering city dwellers in the 1830s. A more spacious and bucolic cousin of those beacons of the Brooklyn shoreline, Brighton Beach and Coney Island, the Rockaway Peninsula is the southernmost point of Queens and has evolved into a quiet and community-minded seaside neighborhood, with a population of loyal locals at its heart amid the boardwalks and sands. Its name alone seems to evoke its existence in New Yorkers' minds as a place a little beyond, at the farthest reaches of the city, and at the point of its greatest exposure to the ocean.

That exposure meant that in recent years—particularly during Hurricane Sandy in 2012—Rockaway bore the brunt of devastating tropical storms, in the aftermath of which the destruction of its historic boardwalks was the least of the area's problems. However, so beloved is Rockaway by the city at large, and so charged with emotion were its inhabitants and neighbors following the storm, that the peninsula has been bouncing back to life, with the city supporting the redevelopment of the famous beachfront eateries, bars, and promenades, and strengthening the iconic boardwalks in the process. Even as it recovers, Rockaway is a wonderful part of the city to visit and a surprisingly seductive corner of the five boroughs.

First, there are the views: Rockaway is a relatively narrow stretch of land, so you can stroll along the Atlantic and face the ocean or walk along the inland side and gaze across Jamaica Bay at Queens and the city skyline beyond. Then there are the beaches themselves: clean sands with treacherous rocky outcrops that make the waves here fun, dramatic, and dangerous—and the only ones in the city to attract the sexy surfing crowd. There are the boardwalks, which wend around the beaches and are dotted with small parks to picnic in and benches to cozy up on in the cool evening sea breeze. And hidden among the boardwalks and the streets are some classic spots for food and drink. Get hot dogs and milkshakes at **Rippers** (*98-1 Shore Front Parkway, at Beach 86th Street; www.86badvibes.com*), the airy and open diner on the oceanfront side, where people congregate in the kind of *Happy Days* atmosphere that makes you feel like you've strolled right back into the 1950s. Walk inland to **DiCosmo's Italian Ice** (*95-19 Rockaway Beach Boulevard, at Beach 96th Street; www.dicosmos.com*) for a true taste of old New York, with the kinds of simple, old-fashioned flavors you'd never think to try from a Häagen-Dazs, and see if you can get to the bottom of your cones before you get back to the beach.

For a day trip out to the Rockaways to feel like a romantic adventure, all you have to do is go with someone you feel passionate about. Whether you choose to head over to Jacob Riis Park, where the beach tends to be a little quieter and more family-oriented, or head in the opposite direction down the peninsula toward the slightly more louche sands of Fort Tilden, we suggest you leave ample time to walk or cycle around, explore the pretty streets, and compare the beaches on either side. And whether you drive out or enjoy the view from the A train, you should go with an inquisitive spirit and enjoy the simple pleasures the peninsula affords—because there aren't many cities in the world that can take you from somewhere like Manhattan to somewhere like Rockaway and back in a day. *Subway: A to Broad Channel; Rockaway Park Shuttle to Beach 90th Street or Beach 98th Street.*

GOVERNORS ISLAND

This 172-acre island less than half a mile from lower Manhattan has blossomed into a perfect summer escape during the relatively short time it's been open to the public. In pre-Colonial times, the island was called Pagganack, or Nut Island, by members of the Manhattan tribe who used it as a fish camp, in honor of the hickory, oak, and chestnut trees that thrive there. The strategically located island passed through the hands of the Dutch and the British (twice), who renamed it Governors Island in 1784. After the Revolution, control of the island was returned to the Americans, and in 1800, New York State handed it over to the U.S. military, which used it for various military functions throughout the first half of the twentieth century. In the early 1900s, the size of the island was increased from 70 to 170 acres using landfill from the construction of the Lexington Avenue subway line, and in the 1920s, the military hired the esteemed architecture firm McKim, Mead & White (designers of the New York Public Library and the Washington Square Park Arch) to build a barracks. Since 2003, the island has belonged to the people of the city of New York, having been sold to the city by the U.S. government for $1. Today, Governors Island is a summer playground, the city's collectively owned backyard, and a seasonal destination for art, recreation, and relaxation buffered from the hectic energy of the city by lapping river water. The island hosts a varied roster of events during the season (it's open seven days a week from Memorial Day weekend through the end of September), such as concerts, chamber music, the New York City Poetry Festival, vintage baseball, and the popular Jazz Age Lawn Party, a gin-soaked gala with Big Band performances and Gatsby-era activities that takes over the island for two weekends every summer. But perhaps the most charming facet of this island oasis is that it's also the perfect place to come for no reason. Easy to reach (by a quick gratis ferry ride from either Manhattan or Brooklyn) but blessed with a sense of escape by virtue of its seclusion, Governors Island is both a unique only-in-New-York attraction and a peaceful counterpoint to the rest of the Big Apple. Bring a picnic (or buy a ready-made one from the Perfect Picnic kiosk), and choose your own special patch of grass for an afternoon of unencumbered leisure. **N.B.:** If you want to pop the question in a private spot that still feels classically New York, we can think of no better locale. Along the island's peaceful perimeter, you'll have your pick of backdrops, from the Statue of Liberty to the Manhattan skyline. *Governors Island is located a half-mile south of Manhattan, and is open to the public seven days a week from late May through late September. Ferries leave every half-hour starting at 10:00 a.m. from the Battery Maritime Building in Manhattan and from Pier 6 in Brooklyn Bridge Park in Brooklyn. Subway: 1 South Ferry, R to Whitehall Street, or 4, 5 to Bowling Green in Manhattan; 2, 3, 4, 5 Borough Hall or R to Court Street in Brooklyn. www.govisland.com.*

CITY ISLAND

As much as New Yorkers like to point out that Manhattan itself is an island, it's often only in crossing the bridges from one borough to another, or in ferrying past the Statue of Liberty, or in spending a happy afternoon at one of Brooklyn's beaches, that one remembers just where New York City is: on the coast of the Atlantic Ocean. City Island, floating in Eastchester Bay off the coast of Pelham in the Bronx, is one of the very few places in the city that still looks and feels like a New England seaside town—and it's one of the city's littlest-known and most charming secrets.

Settled centuries ago by an Englishman named Thomas Pell (for whom one of the small old streets in Chinatown is named), City Island began its development as farmland close to settlements along the Long Island Sound in the seventeenth century. Later, in the eighteenth century, grand plans were drawn up for the island to serve as a new port to the city, where docks and shipyards would rival those that grew up around New York Harbor (where the Statue of Liberty welcomes ships to this day). But after the costs of the Civil War waylaid those plans, City Island was left to develop its own industry from its local resources, slowly becoming a fishing village in the midst of the city's outer boroughs.

Although City Island is very much an active part of New York City—a regular neighborhood, like any other—it's so isolated and has remained unchanged for so long that visiting it is like traveling not only to a different place but also to a different time. This is a town with one main street, a long avenue where you can find everything from the single pharmacy on the island to small art galleries and several inviting restaurants and bars. Head in any direction away from the main drag, and you'll find yourself walking toward the shore, with beaches and docks on all sides offering amazingly bucolic views back to the greenery of Pelham Bay Park, out across the sound to the landscape of Long Island, and as far as the shores of Connecticut.

Increasingly popular as a location for movie shoots, City Island is a beautiful and surprising place to discover, with ornate Victorian houses unlike any you'll find in the rest of the city. It's small enough to explore in a day and quiet enough that you'll never feel crowded there. Head out on the 6 train in the afternoon, and spend a couple of hours walking around the island's beaches, taking in the views over the water, and seeing what kinds of eccentric mansions you can discover. Dip into the **Nautical Museum** (*190 Fordham Street, between Minnieford and King Avenues; www.cityislandmuseum.org*) for a brief taste of City Island culture, and then take your pick of the handful of authentic seafood institutions that line City Island Avenue. Try a fish supper at **Johnny's Reef** (*2 City Island Avenue*), followed by crème brûlée from the **Black Whale** (*279 City Island Avenue, between Carroll and Hawkins Streets; theblackwhalefb. wix.com/theblackwhaleci*) and a stroll along the waterfront at sunset. You'll feel like you've taken someone special on a trip up to New England without ever leaving the city. *City Island is located in Long Island Sound near Pelham Bay Park in the Bronx. Subway: 6 to Pelham Bay Park; take the BX29 bus to the island.*

ART OUTSIDE THE (CITY) LIMITS

From Titian's *Venus and Adonis* in the Met to Robert Indiana's *LOVE* sculpture at Sixth Avenue and West 55th Street, art and romance are publicly and permanently intertwined in the very fabric of New York. Isaac meets Mary for the first time at the Guggenheim in Woody Allen's *Manhattan*, and Harry asks Sally out to the movies in the Egyptian wing of the Met. Couples stroll around the galleries of Chelsea, lovers arrange to meet by the many monuments of the city's sculptured landscape, and there is even romance to be found in the mosaics on the subway walls.

But like love, art exists even beyond the limits of the five boroughs. Manhattan, remember, is situated at the mouth of one of the most beautiful rivers on the continent, surrounded by a natural landscape breathtaking enough to have inspired its own school of romanticist painters. In the peaceful countryside of upstate New York and New Jersey, there is space enough for some of the largest collections of sculpture on display anywhere in the world. And up the Hudson, the cultured sensibility of the city blends seamlessly with the quieter environment in the form of a minimalist museum that gives subtler masterpieces the room they need to be best appreciated. So branch out a little, spend a day away from the hordes, and open your loved one's eyes to the world of art outside the city limits.

DIA:BEACON. This contemporary art museum is a beloved day trip for art-loving New Yorkers, the attractive product of a sensitively designed center for masterpieces of late twentieth-century art and a beautiful, oh-so-accessible location. Perched on the banks of the Hudson River and within walking distance of the Metro-North train station, Dia:Beacon could not be easier to reach, nor a more pleasant urban escape. In Beacon, shops and cafés that would be at home in Williamsburg, Brooklyn, line the main street, while the museum grounds themselves are full of lush nooks and postcard vistas that are a perfect backdrop for a picnic or cozy respite. (If you visit the museum in autumn, you'll be treated to an extra dose of light and color, courtesy of the foliage from the trees that flank the river.) The building, which was converted into a museum after its former life as a Nabisco box-printing factory, impresses those who have recently been confined to the city with a glorious expansiveness of light. The galleries, which are designed to each present the work of a single artist, are airy and ample. In fact, the museum is called a "daylight" museum, as it was designed specifically so that visitors could experience the art in natural light. Make the most of your escape from the great metropolis by approaching the museum via the walkway, which takes you on a quick highlight tour of Hudson Valley scenery. And speaking of scenery, if you're taking the train up, be sure to grab a seat on the left side, the best spot for idyllic, we're-not-in-the-city-anymore views. **N.B.:** Metro-North offers a combined getaway ticket that includes round-trip train fare from the city and admission to the museum for a discounted price (visit www.mta.info/mnr/html/getaways/outbound_diabeacon.htm for details). *Hours vary seasonally. Dia:Beacon is an 80-minute train ride from Grand Central Terminal, and trains leave approximately every hour. 3 Beekman Street, Beacon, New York. 845-440-0100. www.diaart.org/sites/main/beacon. Train: Metro-North Railroad Hudson Line to Beacon.*

STORM KING ART CENTER. This immense outdoor museum contains over one hundred post–World War II sculptures by modern masters including Alexander Calder, Henry Moore, Richard Serra, and Mark di Suvero, as well as installation and other large-scale non-sculptural works by artists such as Andy Goldsworthy and Maya Lin. Storm King is a perfect local counterpoint to the more modestly sized museum treasures located an hour to the south. With so much space to breathe (the park measures about 500 acres), Storm King allows immense pieces of work to stun in their grandness, while at the same time reminding visitors of the art's comparative smallness relative to the expansiveness of nature. For getting around the immense grounds, there are a few options. There's a tram and bike rentals within the park; both are useful if you want to see as much of the park as possible (or if you are trying to combine your trip with a visit to **Dia:Beacon**, which is about a half hour's drive away). But if you've got good shoes and no place to rush off to, try taking Storm King by foot, with the map in your back pocket. The park is really at its best when you allow yourself to forget the hour and the itinerary and instead wander from sculpture to sculpture, watching each piece preen and shift in the light of the day. There's also plenty of privacy, even on the most beautiful days, for pauses and picnics (bring your own, or buy a sandwich from the on-site café) and long conversations about the relationship between art and nature, and the intersection of man-made and natural beauty. *Storm King is open season-*

ally from April to December. A direct bus to Storm King leaves from Port Authority; visit www. coachusa.com for schedules and information. It is about an hour's drive by car from Manhattan. 1 Museum Road, New Windsor, New York. 845-534-3115. www.stormking.org.

GROUNDS FOR SCULPTURE. An hour outside the city, Grounds for Sculpture is a museum in the open air and a beautiful garden where works of art appear as naturally as trees in the landscape. A counterpoint to Storm King upstate, Grounds for Sculpture is west of the city in New Jersey, far enough from the Hudson and the ocean that the only water here is found in the lakes and ponds dotted around the gardens. Less rugged and rural than the country upriver from the city, this is a beautifully and carefully landscaped garden with considered plantings that give each area of the park its own character, like a series of vignettes in a botanical theater. Rather than focusing on the classics and decorating the grounds with works by the most famous sculptors, Grounds for Sculpture aims to open people's eyes to more experimental contemporary artists—so you'll move from bold, abstract pieces emerging from manicured lawns to series of narrative installations hidden in the foliage. A walk around the grounds has all the casual, quiet romance of a stroll around any pretty park—but with the addition of a tactile and seductive sense of adventure. With a frequently changing roster of works on loan supplementing its permanent collection, Grounds for Sculpture is worth visiting more than once, and strolling the grounds on a cool afternoon in the fall is every bit as romantic as buzzing around the flowers in the flush of spring. *126 Sculptors Way, Hamilton, New Jersey. 609-586-0616. www. groundsforsculpture.org. Train: New Jersey Transit from Penn Station to Hamilton. Grounds for Sculpture is a five-minute taxi ride from the train station.*

HUDSON RIVER SCHOOL ART TRAIL. New York is rightly celebrated as one of the capitals of the arts in the world. From the galleries of Chelsea to the grand institutions of Museum Mile and every kind of studio space in between, the city has been home to some of the greatest artists in living memory and the resting place of some of the single most important works ever created. What is less commonly known, though, is that the Hudson River Valley, upstream from Manhattan, was also the inspiration for an entire movement of American art. As the city grew in the early eighteenth century, its inhabitants explored the surrounding countryside, and artists who traveled up to the Catskill Mountains discovered landscapes and scenery that simply had not been seen, much less painted, before. In the words of artist Thomas Cole, after he walked there in the 1830s, "All nature here is new to art."

Nearly two centuries later, the Hudson River School is known as one of the first original American art movements, and the works of its protagonists did for the American landscape what those of John Constable or Vincent van Gogh did for its European counterparts. Artists such as Frederic Church, George Inness, and Cole immortalized the dramatic countryside of the Hudson Highlands, the lakes, and the river itself. Among their preoccupations was the idea of the perfect view, and several of the painters went out of their way to build themselves workshops or even homes in places that would allow them to set up an easel at the ideal vantage point from which to survey the country before them. In so doing, they remain responsible for defining the features for which the Hudson Valley is beloved even today.

The Hudson Highlands and the river valley itself are stunning surroundings for an afternoon's walk, and following in the footsteps of the artists means you can find yourself at some of the most picturesque outlooks in all of New York state. Explore the town of Catskill and the area around **Thomas Cole's home** *(218 Spring Street, Catskill, New York; www.thomascole.org)*, where you can also tour his studio and

Bear Mountain Bridge in the Hudson Valley

see the very scenes he painted from his windows; and then stop by Frederic Church's grand estate at **Olana** (*5720 Route 9G, Hudson, New York; www.olana.org*) before heading off into the relative wilds of the **Catskill Creek**. Or try the east side of the river, and see some of the most dramatic scenery around **Kaaterskill Falls** and **Sunset Rock**, where Cole and Sanford Gifford, among others, turned the craggy wilds into icons of the American romantic landscape.

The beauty of the **Hudson River School Art Trail** is that it's as enjoyable for an art lover as it is for anybody who simply enjoys being out in the country-side. The amazing fact is that just beyond the limits of the five boroughs exists some of the most breathtaking scenery in the state, not to mention the country, and that taking a day to roam around the river and its surrounding hills can be a wonderfully romantic and inspiring break from the city. The trail's website is tremendously helpful, not only in giving careful directions to the various sites of interest, but also in pointing out where to find particular views and the scenes of particular paintings. So we'd suggest you take a look online and figure out which locale you'd like to explore, pack a picnic, and head off early in the morning. The Hudson River School artists were preoccupied with romance in the grandest sense, and—whether it's a gentle hike through the hills, a picnic by the river, or the care-ful discovery of the artists' spots themselves—a walk along the trail is sure to be as seductive now as it ever was. *For this excursion, renting a car will likely be necessary. www.hudsonriverschool.org.*

ESCAPE ITINERARIES

Something that all New Yorkers will say if asked is that coming back to the city—driving back down from upstate, rolling down the railway tracks toward Grand Central, or even watching the city draw nearer from the window of a cab back from the airport—is one of the best things in the world. This is a city that people love as much as they love anything else, and a place people love coming back to the way they love coming back to their loved ones. But to have that feeling, you have to leave in the first place—and believe it or not, there are perfect reasons to get out of the city and wonderfully romantic things to do when you're brave enough to leave the bright lights behind.

Something amazing about New York City is that it contains, in microcosm, such a wide variety of things that might otherwise define an entire coastline or coun-try. It has its own beaches, its own rivers and rivieras; it has some of the finest food and drink in the world, some of the most beautiful parks and green spaces. And the city embraces and reflects the seasons, from ice rinks under the stars in winter to roller derbies in the park in summer. But what you'll find as you travel beyond the city is that the surrounding areas—moving up the coast, up the Hudson, or crossing into Long Island, upstate New York, New Jersey, and Connecticut—contain all those things and more, on a grander scale.

With that in mind, we've suggested here some itineraries for romantic escapes that take you and a loved one out of the city—not into the unknown but into day trips and weekend breaks that make the most of the magical combination of nature and culture that emanates from New York. Within a couple of hours of the city, there are beaches that are the envy of the country, farm-to-table restaurants that lead the world in the slow food revolution, and some of the most acclaimed vineyards on the East Coast. If you are here for more than just a few days and have the means to get out of town one way or the other, these little escapes can be anything from an intimate day away from the bustle to a romantic opportunity to pop the question.

BLUE HILL AT STONE BARNS

It's possible to live in the city for years and never run out of romantic places to go out to eat—New York is simply one of the great culinary capitals of the world. And for many who love living here, the discovery of the most beautiful and serene oasis amid the unrelenting urban noise is the very definition of romantic dining in the city. But thirty miles up the Hudson, New Yorkers can find serenity of an altogether different kind.

Housed within the Stone Barns Center for Food and Agriculture in Pocantico Hills, just outside of Tarrytown and Sleepy Hollow, Blue Hill is one of New York state's great culinary treasures. The younger but nobler sibling of the small and legendarily good restaurant that shares its name in the West Village, Blue Hill at Stone Barns fulfills the ideal of the farm-to-table ethos: there are tours around the center in the daytime and meals made from only the freshest produce in the evenings. Taking its ingredients from local farms (and many from the fields at its very doorstep), the restaurant serves a continually changing seasonal menu and pairs wines to accompany whichever combinations of earthy and fresh ingredients happen to be in season. A visit in the springtime might mean a course of local lamb and fresh mint, served with a chilled French red wine; a trip back up the river in the summer could mean lobster from their farm out in Maine and a crisp Long Island white.

Now among the best-known and most highly acclaimed restaurants in the country, Blue Hill at Stone Barns is expensive and requires reservations long in advance. But the food and wine are only part of the draw—much of the appeal is to be found in the simplicity of the escape to somewhere that's so close but feels so distant from the city. While there are plenty of suitably charming bed-and-breakfasts and hotels around Tarrytown for those who wish to make a weekend of it, perhaps the greatest attraction of Stone Barns is that it's remarkably accessible from Manhattan. A night out upstate is glamorous, romantic, and bucolic all at once; you can catch a train from Grand Central that runs directly along the Hudson to Tarrytown, step into a taxi, and be at Stone Barns in just under an hour. And the moonlight dancing on the river all the way back to the grandeur of midtown will be almost as beautiful as the view from the restaurant's windows. Everybody loves a taste of the country once in a while. *630 Bedford Road, Tarrytown, New York. 914-366-9600. www.bluehillfarm.com. Train: Metro-North Railroad Hudson Line to Tarrytown, then a taxi from the station.*

THE HAMPTONS

From Gordon Gekko's fictitious beach house to the Edies' Grey Gardens, the Hamptons have long been an almost mythical place of escape for New Yorkers with the means to do so. In many ways, the Hamptons are for New York what Cannes or Nice once were for Paris: the destination of choice for well-to-do urbanites looking to bring the glamour of the city to the beauty and tranquility of the waterfront. Where New Yorkers have the edge, however, is in the eternally surprising fact of the geography of Long Island. The South Fork, along whose idyllic southern shore the various towns and villages of the Hamptons are arranged, is only 100 miles from Manhattan.

Romance appears to us in many forms, from picturesque ideals of candlelit dinners and starlit proposals to the triumphs of passion over circumstance. While the Hamptons provide the means and the setting for a romantic break of any kind, our recommendation is to resist the impulse (cultivated in the city) to rush for tables at the best-reviewed restaurants in town, or dress to the nines for cocktails at a sexy nightclub. Instead, the most enjoyable way to spend time in the Hamptons is to embrace what is at the very heart of their appeal: this is a beach vacation, a time for sun and surf and sand and everything that goes with it.

Whether you're heading out east for a weekend in a bed-and-breakfast or you've rented a cottage for a whole week in the summer, the Hamptons make up an entirely new world that's worth exploring over time. Each town and village beyond Hampton Bays—from Southampton to Bridgehampton, Sagaponack, East Hampton, Sag Harbor, Shelter Island, Amagansett, and Montauk—has its own character, which reveals itself in the style and grandeur of the architecture, the number and quality

of the restaurants, and the demographics of the population. Generally speaking, the beaches are quietest around Sag Harbor and Amagansett and busiest around East Hampton and Montauk, which are the trendiest areas and the most popular among the celebrity and socialite sets. But with the simplest expectations, it's almost impossible to go wrong. These are all charming towns that are close enough to the beautiful white beaches that you can feast on fresh seafood or enjoy the spectacle of socialites in town and be back on the sand within minutes.

Of course, there are places to eat and drink in the Hamptons that bring the sophistication of the city to the seaside, and which will always make for a wonderful night. **Ruschmeyer's** *(161 Second House Road, Montauk; www.kingandgrove.com/ montauk-hotels/ruschmeyers)* in Montauk is one of the most fashionable restaurants on the South Fork, inviting guest chefs to spend the summer away from their Manhattan kitchens and to make a summertime menu here instead—the chefs behind Fat Radish and Smile have done so most recently. The outposts of classic Manhattan restaurants like the **Palm** *(94 Main Street, East Hampton; www.thepalm. com)* in East Hampton or **Delmonico's** *(268 Elm Street, Southampton; www.delmonicosrestaurantgroup.com)* in Southampton are, if anything, more exclusive than their urban cousins, with the weight of their menus leaning slightly more toward surf than turf in the summer months. And restaurants such as Tom Colicchio's at **Topping Rose House** *(2546 Montauk Highway, Bridgehampton; www.toppingrosehouse.com)* in Bridgehampton bring a chic and contemporary city sensibility to the pastoral environments of the smaller towns.

But for a true Hamptons experience, we'd suggest something a little more dressed down. Look beyond the bigger names and fancier venues to the local institutions that have been catering to the whims and appetites of seasiders for decades. As unglamorous as it may sound, a humble breakfast of coffee and doughnuts from **Dreesen's** *(15 Lumber Lane, East Hampton; www.dreesens.com)*, the legendary bakers, is as indulgent a way to start the day as any rich plate of eggs Benedict. After breakfast, head out to the sand and spend a day on beaches as beautiful as any in the world, with waves that dwarf the ones the city surfers ride out at Rockaway. The Hamptons beaches are consistently gorgeous, but the key to making a romantic day of it is finding a quiet spot, so we suggest driving along the strip between Amagansett and Montauk, where only the occasional mansion hidden behind the dunes interrupts the peaceful shoreline. For lunch, pull up a seat at the **Clam Bar at Napeague** *(2025 Montauk Highway, Amagansett; www.clambaronline.com)*, where tucking into paper plates of fresh clams and lobster rolls with fresh lemonade will taste better than

The Windmill at Water Mill, outside of Bridgehampton

champagne and caviar. And for dinner, head to **Bostwick's Chowder House** *(277 Pantigo Road, East Hampton; www.bostwickschowderhouse.com)*, where authentic chowder and amazing fresh crab and fish dishes masquerade as comfort food. What could be more romantic than sharing champagne and shellfish at sunset, with the salt of the sea and the sand of the beach still in your hair?

With restaurants, hotels, bed-and-breakfasts, and cottage rentals opening, expanding, and changing every year, the best thing to do concerning lodging is explore online and book as early as you can. The Hamptons are tremendously popular every year as a summer escape for thousands of New Yorkers. And choosing how to get out there is almost as important a part of a Hamptons break as choosing the place to spend your time. Leaving aside the more extravagant options of private helicopter or seaplane from the East River, there are three more accessible options. You can drive yourself, which of course is usually the preferred method given the choice; the only drawbacks are the unpredictability of traffic (especially on weekends) and the difficulty in peak season of finding parking near certain popular beaches, particularly in the busier areas of East Hampton and Southampton. (You'd also need to obtain a town beach pass to park at the beaches themselves; many hotels and rental cottages provide these for guests, but it's worth investigating in advance.) You can go by bus, either on the ever-popular **Hampton Jitney** *(www.hamptonjitney.com)* or the **Hampton Luxury Liner** *(www.hamptonluxuryliner.com)* services, which both take around three hours to get out to the arm of the island beyond East Hampton. Or you can take the **Long Island Rail Road** *(lirr42.mta.info)* from Penn Station, which affords a beautiful view along the coast but sadly shares few of the trappings of decadence with which Gatsby's guests would have traveled a century ago. Our suggestion would be to rent a car yourself for the weekend, since doing so would allow you the freedom to explore the South Fork a little more while you're out there. If a car is not an option, then we'd recommend the train, for the tradition and heritage of the well-traveled rail to and from Penn Station, and staying somewhere central to one of the towns, as close to the beaches as you can find.

WINE AND CYCLING ON THE NORTH FORK

The North Fork is another one of Long Island's getaway destinations, one that runs parallel but at a markedly different frequency than the Hamptons. If you were to hold up two fingers and turn them ninety degrees away from your body, you'd have the shape of Long Island, with the town of Riverhead sitting at the base of your two fingers, the Hamptons running along on your middle finger, and the North Fork on the top, represented by your index finger. The North and South Forks are like fraternal twins, sharing similar geographic traits (flat terrain, surrounded by water) but with noticeable variations. Instead of smooth ocean beaches, the North Fork has the craggy nooks of Peconic Bay and the Long Island Sound. Instead of mansions, there are strawberry patches. Fishing, farming, and viniculture are more prominent here, with the North Fork possessing forty-seven of the sixty vineyards on Long Island and the majority of its farms. The agricultural and fishing traditions have been a part of this area since pre-Colonial times; winemaking started in the 1970s on land that was converted from potato plantings to grape growing.

One of the appealing aspects of both the North and South Forks for visitors from New York City is that, in addition to the sea-splashed beauty of the surroundings, they are both easy to reach from the city without a car. The North Fork in particular lends itself to a day or a weekend of vehicle-less country ambling, especially if you are up for touring by bicycle. You can bring your own on the train (*a $5 permit*

A vineyard on the North Fork of Long Island

is required; www.mta.info/lirr/about/bicycles) or Hampton Jitney, or rent one upon arrival from a company such as **Dan's Bike Rental** *(greenportbikerental.com)*, whose owner will deliver bikes (including helmet, lock, and area map) to any train station or bus stop on the North Fork. Because this area is long, flat, and very narrow, you really have only one decision to make for your route: start east and go west, or start west and go east. Whichever you decide, look for Route 25, a mellow thoroughfare with a specially designated bike shoulder, along which many of the best tourist-friendly wineries, farms, and orchards are located. Most of the vineyards are family-owned and many have tasting rooms, where you can relax and sample (or spit, depending on the hour and how many miles you still have to ride). Some will also allow you to picnic on the grounds. Notable stops include **Sparkling Pointe** *(39750 Country Road 48, Southold; www.sparklingpointe.com)*, which is dedicated to romance-friendly sparkling wines and champagne; **Croteaux Vineyards** *(1450 South Harbor Road, Southold; www.croteaux.com)*, a small vineyard that specializes in rosé and which also has a beautiful tasting area in a converted nineteenth-century barn with a terrace that overlooks the vines; **Lenz Winery** *(38355 New York 25, Peconic; www.lenzwine.com)*, one of the oldest North Fork wineries, which makes some of the most sophisticated wines in the region; and **Shinn Estate** *(2000 Oregon Road, Mattituck; www.shinnestatevineyards.com)*, the best-known vineyard on the North Fork. Consider making this Mattituck winery the last stop on your tour, as it's a place you'll want to linger at (and should you desire to linger past sunset, there is a converted farmhouse on-site with four lovely guest rooms, the price of which includes a delicious breakfast). On Route 25, just west of Jamesport, you'll also pass **Harbes Farm Stand** *(715 Sound Avenue, Mattituck; www.harbesfamilyfarm.com)*, known for its fresh roasted corn, and **Trimble's of Corchaug Nursery** *(20985 Main Road, Cutchogue; www.trimblesnursery.com)*, where you can find a secluded (and sober) spot to relax in the Idea Garden, a peaceful cultivated garden that welcomes visitors. The ride between Jamesport and Greenport is just under twenty miles; the tip of the island, at Orient Point, is another five to eight miles east of Greenport.

If wining and cycling is not your thing, you can also have a romantic journey on the North Fork by touring one of its charming towns. Love Lane in the town of Mattituck is, as its name suggests, a charming destination worth a detour. **Love Lane Kitchen** *(240 Love Lane, Mattituck; www.lovelanekitchen.com)* is a casual all-day dining spot beloved by locals. Or compose your own romantic picnic at the **Village Cheese Shop** *(105 Love Lane, Mattituck; www.thevillagecheeseshop.com)* and bring it over to one of the local picnic areas. Mattituck also hosts an annual strawberry festival each June, a sweet all-town party that culminates in the crowning of the strawberry queen. If you don't want to quite get away from it all, Greenport is the North Fork's most bustling town, with many cafés, boutiques, and antiques stores to explore, as well as a pretty waterfront park with an antique carousel that is a popular destination for couples of all ages at night. If you have a bike or a car and want to explore even further, there's the town of Cutchogue (where Albert Einstein spent several summers contemplating relativity on his little sailboat), Orient and Orient Point (so named because they're the easternmost points of the North Fork), and of course, the beaches. On the North Fork, you've got the choice of either the bay or the sound; the beaches on the sound are rockier but more expansive; the bay is smaller and calmer.

If you are staying the night, the North Fork has a number of new (or newly renovated) inns and boutique hotels, most notably the **North Fork Table and Inn** (*57225 Main Road, Southold; www.nofoti.com*) and the **Greenporter** (*326 Front Street, Greenport; www.greenporterhotel.com*), which is the best bet for those traveling by train or bus, since it's right in the center of town. Though the prices at any of these are quite a bit less than what you'd pay for a room on the South Fork, an even more modest option is overnighting in one of the area's older mom-and-pop operations. **The Mattituck Motel** (*2150 Bay Avenue, Mattituck; www.mattituckmotel.com*) is owned by a local couple who will do everything they can to make your stay easier. And at **Silver Sands** (*1400 Silvermere Road, Greenport; www.silversands-motel.com*), the lack of glitzy amenities is compensated for by its stretch of private beach, with a view of Shelter Island, which sits in between the North Fork and the Hamptons.

SEASIDE ROMANCE IN CONNECTICUT

Home to beaches, seafood, and one of the nation's largest maritime museums, Mystic, Connecticut, is the closest traditional New England seaside destination to the city. Once the home of the Pequot Indians, then Dutch and English settlers, Mystic is a quaint historic town set along the Mystic River and Long Island Sound. **The Inn at Mystic** (*3 Williams Avenue, Mystic; www.innatmystic.com*) is a Colonial Revival estate where Humphrey Bogart and Lauren Bacall spent their honeymoon in 1945. The inn consists of several buildings on a fifteen-acre estate built on a hillside overlooking Mystic Harbor. Lovebirds will want to select the Mansion, whose luxurious suites, filled with period furnishings and boasting exquisite views of the water, orchards, and waterfalls on the grounds, are reserved for adult couples only. While in town, stop for a bite at **Mystic Pizza** (*56 West Main Street, Mystic; www.mysticpizza.com*), a local pizza joint whose evocative name inspired the 1988 rom-com, which was also filmed in the area. A short drive away are several wineries that offer tours and tasting rooms.

This area's beachy, rocky climate yields wines that are similar to those produced on the North Fork of Long Island. *Mystic is a two-and-a-half-hour drive from New York City. There are also several Amtrak trains daily from Penn Station.*

LEAF PEEPING ALONG THE PALISADES

It's often noted that New York has given an invaluable gift of skyline views to the riverfront areas of the state to our west; less often do we New Yorkers thank New Jersey for the Palisades, arguably one of our area's most striking natural features. Just over the George Washington Bridge, eminently visible from upper Manhattan, is this dramatic curtain of steep cliffs woven with trees, which, during the fall, light up with the rich hues of the changing leaves.

Certainly, there are places within the five boroughs (Central and Prospect Parks, of course, along with the Botanic Gardens, Wave Hill, the Bronx's Van Cortlandt Park, and Staten Island's Greenbelt) where you can also admire stunning autumn foliage. And it's true that just standing at the edge of Fort Tryon Park gives you a perfect view of the Palisades across the Hudson, as well as the surrounding foliage of the park itself. But between the drama of the cliffs and the water and the enclosed, secluded feeling of the park on the top of them, the experience of actually visiting the Palisades wins for romance and intimacy.

Peak foliage can be a little hard to plan for, as it depends on an alchemy of weather conditions from as early as six months before. But typically in our area, the last two weeks of October are when you see the richest color. There are a number of ways for couples to experience the Palisades, so choose yours by which mode of transportation you prefer, and whether you want to be guided by experts or make your own way. A number of local tour operators offer seasonal Palisades foliage tours; these are typically half-day bus tours that leave from a central location in Manhattan and make their way through Palisades Interstate Park and other spots around the Hudson Valley. Alternatively, you can rent a car, pack a picnic, and make your own way: go over the George Washington Bridge and make a right, following the sign for the Palisades Interstate Parkway. (**N.B.:** It comes up quickly after the bridge, so don't miss it!) From there, you can leisurely drive around the park; be sure to stop at the State Line Lookout, a scenic viewing point with an old-timey gift shop and refreshment kiosk, built in the 1930s by the Works Progress Administration. (*Directions to the park and various lookout points can be found at www.njpalisades.org.*) More athletic couples can join the legions of local weekend warriors for a bike ride across the George Washington Bridge and through the Palisades via route 9W and River Road. It's not a

IN LOVE IN NEW YORK

route for total beginners, but if you have some previous cycling experience, it's worth your while. If you make it all the way through the park and over the state line into Nyack, New York, you can reward yourselves like the locals do: with a coffee and a homemade donut from **Gypsy Donut** *(18 North Franklin Street, Nyack; www.gypsydonut. com)*. Maple-glazed bacon is the signature flavor and always on the menu; special seasonal flavors rotate throughout the year. Finally, you can get close-up views of the color and cliffs from the water by taking a half-day boat tour. **Classic Harbor Line** *(Cruises depart from Pier 62 on the Hudson River near West 25th Street, in Manhattan; www. sail-nyc.com)* offers seasonal foliage tours along the Hudson on their fleet of schooners and yachts. *Palisades Interstate Park runs along the Hudson River from Fort Lee, New Jersey, to the New York–New Jersey border. For more information, directions, and programs, including hours and directions to State Line Lookout and the Lookout Inn, visit www.njpalisades.com.*

Foliage along the banks of the Hudson River

CHAPTER 5

WILL YOU
NEW YORK ME?

I t's been fun up to this point, but now it's time to get serious. Selecting New York as the backdrop for a proposal or a wedding imbues your commitment with the additional blessing of this beloved and storied city (and ensures some pretty amazing pictures as well). In this chapter, we'll show you a range of weddings venues, from classy hotels and famous churches to rooms with a view, historic houses, spaces within museums, and a few event spaces that have specific charitable slants. We've also created a shopping guide that highlights the best and most interesting places within our retail capital to register for gifts and shop for dresses, suits, invitations, and flowers. And if you're just getting started on the journey to matrimony, please have a look at our map of proposal spots on the following spread to give you ideas on where to pop the question.

As you dream up your New York wedding, keep in mind that as a perennially popular wedding destination (and also a densely populated city with plenty of locals tying the knot), New York's wedding venues are universally desirable—so inquire about specific venues as early as possible, and expect the grandest and most iconic settings to command a pretty penny.

OUTDOOR WEDDINGS

Some of the most appealing venues for a visiting couple to be married in are city parks. Central Park and Prospect Park are discussed in detail in this section, but there are hundreds of parks in every corner of the five boroughs, and at most of them, gatherings such as wedding ceremonies are permitted with only a simple, easily obtainable permit from the New York City Department of Parks and Recreation. Getting married in a park is essentially free; the only venue fee is a $25 processing payment for the permit. And with so many different, lovely green spaces all across the city available at so many hours of the day, it's quite easy to arrange a desired time and place. Permits are required if your ceremony is over twenty people; if it will be under twenty people, a permit is not required, although one is still recommended to ensure use of the space you want. (Note that while the permit grants permission for a group to use a specific space at a specific time and only one group will be given permission for that space and time, the permit does not grant private use of the space, so passersby may still be able to walk through.) Permits are also advised for couples who wish to do wedding photo shoots in a park. One could hold a small picnic reception in a park as well, but keep in mind that there are prohibitions on alcohol and restrictions on decorations, tables, and amplified sound. The permit instructions, application, and FAQs can be found on the parks department's website (*www.nycgovparks.org/permits*). Permit applications take between twenty-one and thirty days to process; there is no additional cost to use the space beyond the application fee. Permits are not issued on summer holiday weekends, such as Memorial Day, Independence Day, and Labor Day.

Whether you're planning a wedding in a city park or one of the gardens listed in this section, you'll want to keep the weather in mind. New York has long, hot summers, a beautiful temperate autumn that extends well into October, cold winters, and unreliable springs. Rain is a possibility at any time of the year, though summer and fall are more prone to passing showers and thunderstorms than long dreary bouts of gray, which are more common in springtime. Moving a wedding because of inclement weather generally isn't an option, so if the gamble makes you nervous, look for a spot that has the option of some shelter (such as the Prospect Park Boat House or Picnic House, or the Botanic Garden), just in case.

CENTRAL PARK

Enchanting and singularly New York, Central Park is also a relatively easy and inexpensive place to be married. One can be wed just about anywhere in the park, and with the exception of the Conservatory Garden (more on this on page 151), you will need only a basic permit that is easily obtained from the New York City Department of Parks and Recreation website (see above) for $25. And decorations are taken care of—whether it's flowers or foliage, the natural backdrop of Olmsted and Vaux whispers enduring beauty.

So how does one go about choosing a spot? For many couples—both local and visiting—the place they choose for their ceremony is dictated by personal history in the park. For one couple, it was always going to be the Conservatory Garden, where the bride would take her kindergarten class on field trips every spring and fall. For another couple, who met as runners on one of the many teams that train in the park, the Dene summerhouse, a gazebo-like structure with a view of the running loop,

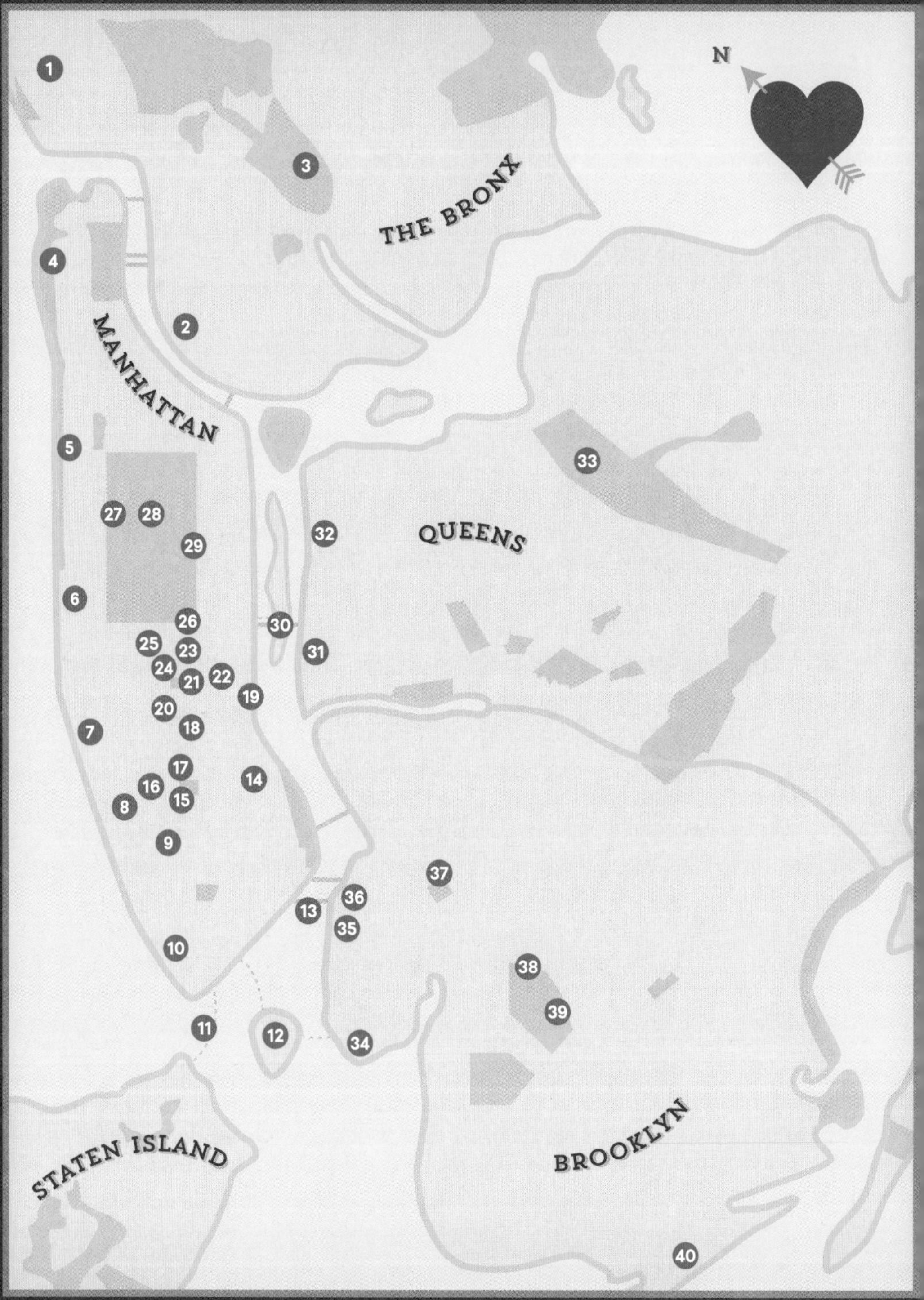
N
THE BRONX
MANHATTAN
QUEENS
STATEN ISLAND
BROOKLYN
1
2
3
4
5
6
7
8
9
10
11
12
13
14
15
16
17
18
19
20
21
22
23
24
25
26
27
28
29
30
31
32
33
34
35
36
37
38
39
40

WHERE TO PROPOSE

1. **The Kerlin Overlook at Wave Hill** *West 249th Street near Independence Avenue*

2. **Yankee Stadium** *East 161st Street and Jerome Avenue*

3. **The Rockefeller Rose Garden at the New York Botanical Garden** *2900 Southern Boulevard*

4. **Fort Tryon Park** *190th Street between Broadway and the Hudson River*

5. **91st Street Flower Garden in Riverside Park** *West 91st Street between Riverside Drive and the Hudson River*

6. **Lincoln Center Plaza** *West 63rd Street between Columbus and Amsterdam Avenues*

7. **The High Line** *Tenth Avenue between Gansevoort and West 30th Streets*

8. **The Gardens at St. Luke's in the Field** *487 Hudson Street between Barrow and Christopher Streets*

9. **In the Cronut line at Dominique Ansel Bakery** *189 Spring Street between Thompson and Sullivan Streets*

10. **Robert Wagner Park** *The Hudson River at Battery Place*

11. **On the Staten Island Ferry** *Between the Whitehall Terminal in Manhattan and the St. George Ferry Terminal on Staten Island*

12. **Governors Island** *Via ferry from Battery Maritime Building, 10 South Street in Manhattan; or (weekends) Pier 6, Brooklyn Bridge Park at Atlantic Avenue*

13. **On the Brooklyn Bridge** *Between Downtown Brooklyn and City Hall in Manhattan*

14. **9th Street Community Garden** *East 9th Street at Avenue C*

15. **Under the arch in Washington Square Park** *Fifth Avenue and Washington Square North*

16. **Stonewall Inn** *35 Christopher Street between Waverly Place and 7th Avenue South*

17. **Washington Mews** *Between University Place and Fifth Avenue just south of East 8th Street*

18. **11 Madison Park** *11 Madison Avenue between 24th and 25th Streets*

19. **Tudor City Park** *Tudor City Place between 42nd and 43rd Streets*

20. **Top of the Empire State Building** *Fifth Avenue at 34th Street*

21. **Astor Hall in the New York Public Library** *Fifth Avenue at 42nd Street*

22. **The Whispering Gallery in Grand Central** *East 42nd Street between Lexington and Vanderbilt Avenues*

23. **Tiffany's** *57th Street at Fifth Avenue*

24. **MoMA Sculpture Garden** *54th Street between Fifth and Sixth Avenues*

25. **The Rink at Rockefeller Center** *West 48th Street between Fifth and Sixth Avenues*

26. **Pulitzer Fountain at Grand Army Plaza** *Fifth Avenue at 59th Street*

27. **Shakespeare Garden** *West side of Central Park around 79th Street*

28. **Turtle Pond** *By the Great Lawn in Central Park between 79th and 80th Streets*

29. **Roof of the Met** *Fifth Avenue between East 80th and East 84th Streets*

30. **On the Roosevelt Island Tram** *From 59th Street and Second Avenue*

31. **Long Island City waterfront** *Gantry Plaza State Park, between 46th and 49th Avenues*

32. **The Noguchi Museum sculpture garden** *33rd Road at Vernon Boulevard*

33. **The Unisphere** *Flushing Meadows Corona Park, northwest end of the park between United Nations Avenue N and United Nations Avenue*

34. **Valentino Pier** *Louis Valentino, Jr. Park, Coffey Street at Ferris Street*

35. **Brooklyn Heights Promenade** *The Esplanade, above the BQE between Joralemon Street and Grace Court*

36. **Jane's Carousel in DUMBO** *Brooklyn Bridge Park at Dock Street*

37. **The monument in Fort Greene Park** *Center of the park, near the Willoughby Avenue entrance*

38. **The Vale of Cashmere in Prospect Park** *Northeast side of the park, near the Grand Army Plaza entrance*

39. **The Prospect Park Boathouse** *Southeast side of the park, near the Lincoln Road and Ocean Avenue entrance*

40. **Coney Island Boardwalk** *Boardwalk between West 37th and Brighton 1st Streets*

had special meaning. Because there are so many options, taking a post-engagement scouting trip with your beloved is the best way to find that special place that suits your vision and personalities, whether it's the breathtaking (but rather exposed) Bow Bridge, the terrace of Belvedere Castle, the beautiful shelter of the Dene summerhouse, the Ladies Pavilion, Cop Cot, Wagner Cove, or the Shakespeare Garden (so named because every flower comes from one of the Bard's plays)—to name just a very few possible locales among the park's 843 acres. Other details to keep in mind are the size of your wedding (some spots in the park can accommodate fewer guests than others, and if you are having more than twenty guests, you are required to get a permit); whether you want a venue with some kind of shelter or benches; and how private you want the space to feel. (Note that a permit only gives you permission to have the ceremony and a gathering within the park; it does not grant private access to a designated space. While only one permit is granted per area per time slot, venues are still technically open to the public.) Another detail to consider is timing: to some couples, having a bit of character will add to the local charm, but if you want to avoid the risk that a brusque New Yorker will be pushing his or her way through your vows, consider scheduling the ceremony during an off time, like a weekday morning. And if your gathering is large enough that you will need a permit, many holiday weekends will be off-limits, as the parks department reserves the space for public use on a first-come, first-served basis.

The one exception to the general protocol—and the most popular place within the park grounds to be married—is the Conservatory Garden at Fifth Avenue near East 105th Street. Here, you can have up to one hundred guests (a larger number than can be accommodated elsewhere in the park), and there is a fee of $400 for exclusive use of the garden for one hour, plus an additional $100 for an optional half-hour photography session with up to twenty-five people. You can hold a wedding here from late spring through early October, and it's best to reserve well in advance, as this is a popular venue for both residents and tourists. *For more information on getting married in the Conservatory Garden, visit www.centralparknyc.org/visit/general-info/weddings/.*

Note that with the exception of privately operated spaces such as the Lakeside Restaurant at the Loeb Boathouse, you can only have a wedding ceremony on park grounds, not a reception (this includes the Conservatory Garden). No alcohol, amplified music, or throwing of rice and confetti is permitted, although live music is okay. The boathouse restaurant, which is one of the city's more popular venues, can be booked by contacting the restaurant directly, either by phone or via a form on the restaurant's website, *www.thecentralparkboathouse.com.*

Links to the permit applications, regulations, and everything you need to know for a basic ceremony are all available online *(www.centralparknyc.org)*; if you would like something more elaborate, agencies which specialize in planning park weddings for visitors such as Wed in Central Park *(www.wedincentralpark.com)* can help secure dates, suggest locations within the park, and coordinate logistics. *Central Park is located from 59th to 110th Streets, between Fifth Avenue and Central Park West. www.centralparknyc.org.*

PROSPECT PARK

Not long after finishing their work for Central Park, Olmsted and Vaux turned their attention to Brooklyn, and in designing Prospect Park they felt they had created their masterpiece. One of the great pastoral landscapes of the period in the country, Prospect Park has been one of Brooklyn's premier attractions for more than a century, and it remains the most beautiful green space in the borough. Vast and varied, with wide-open meadows and quiet woods, man-made hills and carefully considered views, the park is a cornerstone of Brooklyn life year-round, and as such is an increasingly popular venue for weddings for Brooklynites passionate about their borough. While you're free to pose for engagement or wedding photos throughout the park, there are four official sites for weddings, each of which can accommodate between 100 and 150 guests and comes with a choice of exclusive caterers and an eight-hour reservation (with the first two of those hours for setup and the final hour for cleaning).

The two most popular sites for ceremonies within the park are the **Boathouse** and the **Picnic House**. The **Boathouse** is one of Prospect Park's oldest and most beloved buildings, a historic landmark on the shore of the lake toward the easternmost side of the park. Lullwater, as the lake is known, is a beautiful and peaceful pool of green bordered by landscaped gardens, rockeries, and bridges. In the afternoon, light streams in through the boathouse's windows and French doors along the waterfront, making daytime weddings bright and jovial. If you choose an evening wedding, the beautiful old glass lamps along the waterfront and lining the paths cast a golden glow across the lake and mingle with the moonlight on the water.

The **Picnic House** resides in the wooded fringes of the Long Meadow, between Park Slope and Grand Army Plaza, on the opposite side of the park from the boathouse. Like other monuments that define the landscape, it's one of several structures that people who frequent the park have come to recognize without ever really knowing what it's for—in part because, outside of private events, it's closed to the public for most of the year. But the Picnic House is a charming building, red brick on the outside with a clean white interior, and with views that look out across the meadow

and the treetops. In keeping with the intentions of the park's designers, the views from the house are about as close as one can get in Brooklyn to the feeling of being in the countryside, or at least in the landscaped gardens of an English country estate.

Beyond the two larger venues, there are two other locations within the park where weddings are permitted: the **Oriental Pavilion** and the **Grecian Shelter**. While each is a covered structure, they're both open-walled and are therefore better suited for spring and summertime weddings where guests will spend most of their time in the fresh air, and they have slightly smaller capacities. The former has the feel of a pagoda in a Japanese garden and is set in Concert Grove, a shaded part of the park peacefully enclosed by trees. The latter, also known as the Peristyle, is in some ways the most formal and traditional-looking venue, a Palladian colonnade close to the edge of the park with a grand and open feel.

Prospect Park is many things to many people—a place for summer concerts, Fourth of July barbecues, quiet walks, and flying kites—and, with such variety to be found in its venues for ceremonies, it can also be a beautiful and bucolic setting for a Brooklyn wedding. *www.prospectpark.org.*

WILL YOU NEW YORK ME?

GARDENS

Along with the city parks themselves, New York is blessed with some of the most beautiful classically maintained gardens, each of which makes a wonderful setting for a wedding. Events at the Brooklyn Botanic Garden, Wave Hill, or the New York Botanical Garden in the Bronx have the distinction of feeling at once unique to the city and yet removed from the more common routine of city life. While these private gardens may command higher prices and require more careful advance planning than even the iconic Central Park, their advantages lie in the greater sense of privacy and the more personally tailored arrangements that are afforded by their relative exclusivity.

The **Brooklyn Botanic Garden** (*see page 118*) is the most flexible of the formal parks, with a range of options that cater to large or small parties, indoor or out-door ceremonies, and locations throughout the grounds for wedding or engagement photography. Situated adjacent to Prospect Park and beloved by Brooklynites and many from around the five boroughs, the gardens are popular in part for the distinct characters of the various landscapes within its walls. Everybody who has spent time here has his or her favorite spot, and many of the best-loved areas are available for events of one kind or another. Some of the prettiest seasonal gardens are available throughout the year for photography, from the Cherry Esplanade and Bluebell Wood in spring to the Cranford Rose Garden in June and the rambling woods in the fall. The more intimate of the smaller gardens, such as the Osborne Garden, the rose garden, and the Japanese Hill-and-Pond Garden, are available for smaller outdoor ceremonies. And there are two stunning spaces available for indoor ceremonies: the newer Lillian and Amy Goldman Atrium, which overlooks Cherry Esplanade, and the fantastically grand Palm House, the architectural jewel in the garden's crown, a Victorian-style conservatory building with adjacent terraces, fountains, and lawns. *150 Eastern Parkway, between Underhill and Washington Avenues, in Brooklyn. 718-623-7200. www.bbg.org. Subway: 2, 3 to Eastern Parkway–Brooklyn Museum.*

In contrast to the breadth of Brooklyn's park, **Wave Hill**—a private landscaped estate in the Riverdale section of the Bronx—is as intimate as a botanical garden can get. Holding a wedding at Wave Hill requires first the purchase of a year's member-ship at a price of $10,000 (almost all of which is tax-deductible), in addition to the costs of hiring the spaces and working with the exclusive caterers in partnership with the park. But an event here is truly exclusive, and hiring the garden means exactly that—it is only available for evening weddings, after the park has closed to the pub-lic, so you have the entire place to yourselves for the night. While there are limited options for spots around the gardens where a ceremony can take place, the nature of the landscape almost makes the choice for you—after all, when you have the option of a wedding on the Pergola, overlooking the Hudson to the Palisades from the beautifully planted terraces, why would you choose anything else? Wave Hill House itself is both intimate and grand, with views from within that are almost as good as those from the terraces in front, and it makes a spectacular venue for the reception. And there are a number of charming locations available for photography, from the flower gardens to the conservatories and the curious aquatic garden, an Italianate pond surrounded by benches, pagodas, and lush plants that move with the seasons from tropical lilies to wintry hedgerows. But best of all, with the entire landscape at your disposal, it's probably the only chance you'll get to roam the grounds as if they're your own for a night, with nobody else in sight. *675 West 252nd Street, between Sycamore and Independence Avenues, in the Bronx. 718-549-3200. www.wavehill.org. Subway: 1 to Van Cortlandt Park–242nd Street (where the free Wave Hill shuttle bus will pick visitors up and drive them to the gardens; check website for times and details).*

Grandest of all, the **New York Botanical Garden** covers 250 acres in the heart of the Bronx and offers perhaps the most formal backdrop for a landscape wedding. Thanks to its sheer size and its illustrious history as the city's showpiece of landscaping and conservation (which we discuss elsewhere in this book), the NYBG truly combines the beauty of a botanical garden with the identity of the city itself. Both demand and cost for arranging events here are high—the gardens are extremely popular as a location not only for weddings but also for film, photography, and large events of all kinds—but if grandeur and a sense of really belonging to New York are important, it's worth the wait. Whether you're looking for an outdoor ceremony or for indoor arrangements, the garden has a wealth of options that are as intimate and romantic as they are iconic and recognizable. *2900 Southern Boulevard, in the Bronx. 718-817-8700. www.nybg.org. Transportation: Metro-North Railroad Harlem Line to Botanical Garden.*

In addition to the city's most famous parks and gardens, there are some other attractive green spaces where you can have an outdoor ceremony that feels totally New York, but cozier and a little off the beaten path. **Jefferson Market Garden** is one such place. The location isn't at all obscure; it's right in the middle of Greenwich Village, nestled under one of downtown's most distinctive landmarks, the Jefferson Market Library, with its Victorian Gothic clock tower. Still, many New Yorkers don't even realize it's there. The garden sits on a strange peninsula between Sixth and Greenwich Avenues, buffered from the traffic and concealed from sight by iron gates and sound-absorbing foliage. (The "market" in the name comes from the food hall that was the space's original nineteenth-century use.) It was this urban-oasis quality that attracted *Sex and the City*'s Miranda and Steve, who discover it while walking down the street talking about how they can't find a place to get married that feels right. As Miranda complains, saying that every place in New York seems too cheesy for them, their shopping bags break right in front of the garden's gate and they notice, for the first time, this perfect, non-sappy spot. (Or, as Miranda says, "I don't hate it!") The real-life backstory of the garden is even less genteel. In the 1870s, the firm of Vaux and Withers (Vaux being Calvert Vaux, who designed Central and Prospect Parks) designed a courthouse that took over the space that had originally been a market. (The splashiest moment in the court's history was when millionaire Henry K. Thaw successfully pleaded insanity for the murder of architect Stanford White, who had had an affair with Thaw's wife, the chorus girl Evelyn Nesbit.) Adjacent to the courthouse, on the land the garden now occupies, was a women's prison (demolished in 1974), which over the course of several decades counted as residents alleged spy Ethel Rosenberg, black activist Angela Davis, and Valerie Solanas, the schizophrenic feminist who shot Andy Warhol. In the 1960s, the courthouse building was converted into a library (thanks to preservation efforts led by a group that included E. E. Cummings), and in the '70s, community activists successfully wrestled the land that the women's prison had been on into the hands of the city's Department of Parks and Recreation. None of that tumult is visible in the garden today, which is beautifully landscaped, with a lovely koi pond, and for a modest donation can be reserved for wedding ceremonies and photography sessions from April through October. *70A Greenwich Avenue, between Sixth Avenue and West 10th Street, in Manhattan. www.jeffersonmarketgarden.org. Subway: 1 to Christopher Street–Sheridan Square; A, B, C, D, E, F, M to West 4th Street.*

INDOOR WEDDINGS

The range of possibilities for indoor wedding venues is as diverse as the city itself. There are museums, churches, hotels (classic and brand new), historic homes, and private event spaces with skyline views—to name just a few. In this section, we've highlighted a number of options in each of these categories (and a few others) that are appealing aesthetically and historically, but which also may suit the specific needs of visitors. In addition to the options described in this section, many restaurants and bars—from four-star to neighborhood joint—have private rooms or spaces that can be ideal for the small wedding parties of a traveling couple. Even restaurants that do not have dedicated event spaces will sometimes accommodate requests, so if there's a spot that has a special place in your heart, it's worthwhile to contact them to see if they'll be able to suit your needs.

MUSEUMS

In a city that prides itself on its culture as much as New York, it's no surprise that many of its most celebrated institutions are also popular venues for weddings and receptions. For those looking for an iconic indoor New York wedding, the inherent grandeur of these landmarks makes them perfect locations for the big day. And, of course, the range of such places mirrors the breadth of the city's culture, allowing you to choose a venue that is in keeping with your passions—artistic, historic, or otherwise.

The **New York Public Library**'s Stephen A. Schwarzman building *(Fifth Avenue at 42nd Street, in Manhattan; www.nypl.org)*, which borders Bryant Park and constitutes possibly the most beautiful corner of midtown, is a breathtaking space that can be tailored (with the help of your wedding planner) to suit any taste. Impressive marble staircases allow you to make the grandest entrance into its luxurious ballroom, and with some of its oldest rooms available for hire, it makes an excellent venue for smaller ceremonies (civic only) or larger receptions. (However, note that the library has become infinitely more popular since its potential as a venue was illustrated, albeit tragically, in the *Sex and the City* movie.) Uptown on the west side, the **American Museum of Natural History** *(Central Park West between West 77th and 81st Streets, in Manhattan; www.amnh.org)* offers a uniquely New York experience: a beloved location for New Yorkers from childhood to old age, and home to the city's finest collection of dinosaurs and dioramas, the museum opens its doors by night to become a sophisticated venue for extravagant receptions. Events can be divided between the Powerhouse, a large space converted from the museum's former power station into its grandest hall, and the North Galleria, a smaller glass-walled room perfect for predinner drinks or smaller parties. Both offer spectacular views of the Rose Center and Central Park beyond—and, to indulge your beloved's childhood fantasies, private tours of the museum are available as well. The **New-York Historical Society** *(170 Central Park West, between West 76th and 77th Streets, in Manhattan; www.nyhistory.org)* next door, meanwhile, presents an altogether different but equally extravagant experience. Renovated with no expense spared in 2011, the building is now among the best-preserved historic landmarks in the city. By day, the palatial building houses collections of art and hosts cultural events in its many halls and theaters; after hours, the various galleries can be hired separately, for anything from an open reception in the light-filled Smith Gallery to an intimate dinner and a taste of old New York in the Klingenstein Library, bordered by Palladian columns and stained-glass windows.

For an indoor wedding with a view, there are a number of options, from the skyline to Museum Mile and beyond. The **Museum of the City of New York** (*1220 Fifth Avenue, between East 103rd and 104th Streets, in Manhattan; www.mcny.org*)—an underappreciated institution occupying a beautiful Georgian-style mansion at the top end of Museum Mile on Fifth Avenue—is not only one of the most pristine mansions in the city, it also offers some of the most unusual views of Central Park. There are terraces and a courtyard available for outdoor receptions (which can be tented in the winter), and if you follow the winding marble stairs up to the second floor, you'll find the gem at the heart of the museum: a reception hall with windows that look out across Fifth and over the Conservatory Garden and other parts of the park that really can't be seen any other way. All the way downtown, at the southern tip of Manhattan, the **Museum of Jewish Heritage** (*36 Battery Place, in Manhattan; www.mjhnyc.org*) is one of the few venues in the city that offers views of the Statue of Liberty. Ideal for an evening reception, its large dining room has windows that curve around the edge of Battery Park, looking out across New York Harbor to Governors Island, Ellis Island, Lady Liberty herself, and the sunset over New Jersey beyond. And for a real sense of cosmopolitan grandeur, try the **United Nations Delegates Dining Room** (*1 United Nations Plaza, between East 44th and 45th Streets, in Manhattan; www.aramark-un.com*) on the east side of midtown. Visited by thousands of tourists throughout the year and revered as an example of modern International-style architecture, the UN is also surprisingly accessible as a venue for spectacular receptions. The world-famous Delegates Dining Room features floor-to-ceiling windows that overlook the East River, Brooklyn, and Queens, while its terraces (including the new Ambassadors River View terrace) can be used for outdoor receptions and tented in the cooler months.

Across the East River from the terraces of the UN building are two great Brooklyn institutions for the arts: the Brooklyn Museum and the Brooklyn Academy of Music. Having seen major renovations and surges of investment in recent years, both reflect the cultural shift in the city toward Brooklyn—and both can make stunning venues for ceremonies and receptions. The **Brooklyn Museum** (*200 Eastern Parkway, between Underhill and Washington Avenues, in Brooklyn; www.brooklynmuseum. org*) borders Prospect Park and is close to Grand Army Plaza and the Brooklyn Public Library. Mixing majestic older interiors with the clean glass and steel of its more minimal contemporary exterior, the museum feels both glamorous and traditional—a combination that informs its spaces for hire, where you can choose between the smaller, naturally lit, and more modern Rubin Pavilion and the impossibly grand Beaux-Arts Court, with sixty-foot ceilings and details dating back to 1927. Across downtown Brooklyn toward Atlantic Avenue, the **Brooklyn Academy of Music** (*30 Lafayette Avenue, between Ashland Place and St. Felix Street, in Brooklyn; www.bam.org*) is a cultural hub, hosting everything from ballet and opera to independent cinema. But for the month of July—and *only* for the month of July—the Lepercq Space in BAM's main Peter Jay Sharp Building, otherwise used for performances and other cultural events, can be hired for weddings and receptions. An ideal reflection of Brooklyn chic, the space is flooded with light from the stained-glass windows (visible from the street on Lafayette Avenue) and lined with walls of exposed brick, creating a ballroom that feels contemporary, comfortable, and grand at the same time.

RELIGIOUS VENUES

If you desire a traditional religious ceremony for your New York wedding, you're not alone. Rest assured, many couples who come to the city to wed have more than landmarks on their minds, and while holding a ceremony in a place of worship of which you are not a member requires some additional research, it's an easily achievable (and generally affordable) goal. First, some bad news: if you have your heart set on **St. Patrick's Cathedral** (*Fifth Avenue between East 50th and 51st Streets, in Manhattan; www.saintpatrickscathedral.org*), it's probably not going to happen. To be wed at James Renwick Jr.'s Fifth Avenue landmark, you must be a parishioner currently living in the Archdiocese of New York. (Manhattan, Staten Island, and the Bronx are part of the Archdiocese of New York. Brooklyn and Queens comprise the Archdiocese of Brooklyn.) For those who qualify, applications can be submitted to the priest a year prior to your wedding date. The requirements are less stringent at the cathedral's elder sibling, **St. Patrick's Old Cathedral** (*263 Mulberry Street, between Jersey and Prince Streets, in Manhattan; www.oldcathedral.org*), a Gothic Revival basilica just north of Little Italy, so known because it was the seat of the Archdiocese of New York before "new" St. Patrick's opened in 1879. The old St. Patrick's has a different sort of charm, owing to its lower-profile location: rather than looming over the middle of Fifth Avenue, it's tucked into the middle of a SoHo block, set gracefully back from the street. It's a common sight, in fact, for weekend shoppers to turn the corner of Mulberry Street and see a just-married couple posing for photographs on the church steps. To be married here, one need not be a member of the church or a resident of

New York City, but at least one member of the couple must provide baptism records. The interior may ring a bell for fans of *The Godfather*, for it was the location used to shoot the movie's infamous baptism scene.

Prerequisites are less stringent at one of the city's other great ecclesiastical landmarks, **Saint John the Divine** (*1047 Amsterdam Avenue, between West 110th and 113th Streets, in Manhattan; www.stjohndivine.org*), the mother church of the Episcopal Diocese of New York. This immense cathedral (the fourth largest in the world) sits within a large complex in the Morningside Heights neighborhood with several other church buildings and gardens inhabited by three peacocks in residence, Phil, Harry, and Jim. (The peacocks are named for two former clergy members and the former head of the Cathedral School.) There are no membership or baptism requirements to be married at Saint John the Divine, and since 2012, cathedral priests have been performing same-sex weddings here. They perform interfaith ceremonies as well. (Note, however, that to be married here, the church requires that the marriage license be procured from the state of New York and brought to the officiating priest at least a week prior to the wedding.) While the cathedral's immense main chapel is best suited for weddings of more than 200 people and booked well in advance, there are seven side chapels that are good for smaller ceremonies. Known as the Chapels of the Tongues, each is named for a saint representing a region of the world (Germany, Denmark, Ireland and Scotland, Spain, France, Italy, and Africa and the Far East), an homage to the countries from which most immigrants traveled to the United States at the time that the cathedral was built. (It opened in 1899.) Prospective brides and grooms should note that although the church is liberal about who they allow to marry, the facilities book up with many marital and nonmarital events, so if you are interested in being married here, contact the cathedral's special events coordinator as early as possible.

St. Bartholomew's Church (*325 Park Avenue, between East 50th and 51st Streets, in Manhattan; www.stbarts.org*), commonly known as St. Bart's, is a grand Episcopal church in midtown. If you've ever taken a cab from Grand Central up Park Avenue, you've probably noticed its opulent architecture on the east side of the avenue, perhaps noting the tiled dome or the massive portals, which were designed by the architect Stanford White, and bronze doors decorated with biblical scenes. (The beloved doors were originally installed on the church's former building on Madison Avenue; the current structure, erected in the early twentieth century, was designed to accommodate them.) The church is also known for its pipe organ, which is the largest in New York and among the largest in the world. St. Bart's was used in the penultimate scene

of the 1981 romantic comedy *Arthur* as the location of the arranged wedding between Arthur and Susan, the bride deemed suitable by his wealthy family. (After Arthur calls off the wedding, he and his true love, Linda, played by a lithe Liza Minnelli, sit on the altar to plan their penniless future after Arthur is disowned.) An appealing feature of St. Bart's, in addition to the beauty of the church itself, is that there is an on-site restaurant called **Inside Park** *(www.insideparknyc.com)*. The restaurant occupies the church's former social hall; while it feels a bit cavernous at regular mealtimes, it has a nice, churchy character that is well suited for a gathering to celebrate a wedding ceremony. Adjacent to the restaurant is a terrace set a few steps above the street that can be used for a reception or cocktail hour, from which your guests can take in the distinctive grandeur of Park Avenue. To be married at St. Bart's, at least one member of the couple must be a baptized Christian, although membership to St. Bart's is not required. Private events can be held at Inside Park by anyone, regardless of whether a ceremony is held at the church.

While it no longer houses a congregation, no list of the city's religious wedding venues would be complete without mentioning the one-of-a-kind **Angel Orensanz Foundation** *(172 Norfolk Street, between East Houston and Stanton Streets, in Manhattan; www.orensanzevents.com)*. One of the oldest synagogue buildings in New York City, this massive Gothic Revival structure was built in 1849 by a congregation of German Jews for their reform community to worship in. The building ceased to be used as a synagogue in 1974, and it was abandoned and vandalized. Twelve years later, the sculptor Angel Orensanz bought the building and established it as a foundation and a nondenominational venue for the arts. Today, the foundation runs a world-class program of exhibitions and performances (the diverse list of past performers and guests includes Elie Wiesel, Maya Angelou, Florence and the Machine, and the designer Zac Posen, who often holds his fashion shows here) and manages the ongoing maintenance of the historic building. And what a building it is: with an interior that resembles, in places, Notre Dame de Paris, the Sistine Chapel, and Solomon's Temple, with soaring, buttressed ceilings, a great neo-Gothic altar, and two levels of carved-wood balconies, it's no surprise that this is a popular venue for local couples, especially those with ties to the arts. Though it was originally a house of worship, one need not be Jewish to be married in this extraordinary building—among the hundreds of New York City couples who have tied the knot here are Sarah Jessica Parker and Matthew Broderick, who were married by Broderick's sister, an Episcopal priest. **N.B.:** You can hold both the ceremony and reception at the foundation, or one or the other, but given the size, the venue is best suited for larger guest lists.

HOTELS

The indoor counterpoint to a Central or Prospect Park wedding, holding nuptials in one of the city's swank hotels is as classic as it comes. Venues such as the **Plaza** *(768 Fifth Avenue, between West 58th and 59th Streets, in Manhattan; www.theplazany.com)*, the **Pierre** *(2 East 61st Street, between Madison and Fifth Avenues, in Manhattan; www.tajhotels. com/Luxury/Grand-Palaces-And-Iconic-Hotels/The-Pierre-New-York/Overview.html)*, and the **Waldorf Astoria** *(301 Park Avenue, between East 49th and 50th Streets, in Manhattan; www.waldorfnewyork.com)* are irreplaceably iconic, with price tags to match. These are settings for grand affairs (though at the Waldorf, in addition to several grand ballrooms—the largest of which is four stories high—you can also choose to have a seated reception for up to one hundred guests in the hotel's Conrad Suite, where Grace Kelly and Prince Rainier held their engagement party in 1956). Meanwhile, at the legendarily discreet **Carlyle** *(35 East 76th Street, between Park and Madison Avenues, in Manhattan; www.rosewoodhotels.com/en/the-carlyle-new-york)*, you can also have a more intimate version of the classic hotel wedding. While the Carlyle does not have banquet halls, there are several suites (as well as the Café Carlyle restaurant) that can be booked for small- and medium-sized weddings and receptions. And though holding an event of any size at one of these venerable addresses should never be the first choice for true bargain hunters, most include a night's stay for the bride and groom, as well as complimentary or discounted amenities, such as spa treatments.

In addition to these classics, there are two newer hotels that couples who want an intimate wedding celebration should consider. The **NoMad Hotel** *(1770 Broadway, between West 27th and 28th Streets, in Manhattan; www.thenomadhotel.com)*, located on lower Madison Avenue in the upper Flatiron District, is a boutique hotel in an elegant Beaux-Arts building that has won accolades for its restaurant (the chef and owner earned four stars from the *New York Times* at Eleven Madison Park before moving here). There is a private dining room on the top floor with an adjoining rooftop terrace and garden that can be used for wedding ceremonies and receptions. The space can accommodate forty guests for a seated dinner indoors (or eighty with the outdoor space), or a larger number for cocktail receptions. Whether indoors or outdoors, the space has terrific views of Manhattan, including the Empire State Building. Across the river is the **Wythe** *(80 Wythe Avenue, between North 11th and 12th Streets, in Brooklyn; www.wythehotel.com)*, a soaring Williamsburg hotel that epitomizes industrial chic and Brooklyn cool. The building the hotel is housed in was converted from its original purpose, an early twentieth-century barrel-making factory. Though both hotels are modern and luxurious, where the NoMad is plush, dark, and cozy, the Wythe is lighter, with plenty of visible brick and exposed wood. The owner of the Wythe also owns Diner and Marlow & Sons, two pioneers of the neighborhood's notable dining scene, and as at the NoMad, food and drink are at the forefront. The Wythe has a number of event spaces, from a pine-ceilinged banquet hall to a private screening room, but in our opinion, the most desirable are the two lofts on the hotel's glass-enclosed top floor, which offer at once unique intimacy and a signature taste of New York. Each can accommodate up to forty guests for standing gatherings, and one has a private terrace. The floor-to-ceiling windows offer postcard views of Manhattan.

ALL ABOUT THE VIEW

Getting married in a landmark such as Central Park or the American Museum of Natural History is one way to have an unmistakably New York wedding; another is to find a setting with a view. Prioritizing the view rather than the space opens up the pool of potential venues and allows you to shift your planning away from the most famous, most popular, and most expensive local venues. In fact, a good number of NYC couples choose to hold their weddings in rentable loft spaces, which are typically large "raw" spaces (the couple needs to bring in everything) that are all about the vista. Many are located on the far west side of Manhattan, with views overlooking the Hudson; or in DUMBO, with views of Manhattan. The advantage is that these spaces can be cheaper than well-known restaurants and event spaces, and they are more plentiful than famous museums, hotels, and parks; however, at most loft spaces, the fee you pay is for renting the space only, and you will need to rent or bring in anything else you want for your event (flowers, chairs, decorations, catering). The best place to research spaces and availability is *New York Magazine*'s Wedding Guide (available in print and online at www.nymag.com/weddings/), which offers up-to-date listings for loft spaces around the city. Another option is to hold your wedding in one of the waterfront park areas across the Hudson or East Rivers, in either **Liberty State Park** *(200 Morris Pesin Drive, in Jersey City; www.state.nj.us/dep/parksandforests/parks/liberty.html)*, in New Jersey, or **Gantry Plaza State Park** *(4-09 47th Road, in Queens; www.nysparks.com/parks/149/details.aspx)*, in Long Island City. For views from a slightly different vantage point—one that looks at the city from within instead of looking across the water—visiting couples might also consider the bar and event space **230 Fifth** *(230 Fifth Avenue, between West 26th and 27th Streets; www.230-fifth.com)*. Located on the top floors of a Flatiron office building, 230 Fifth has dramatic up-close-and-personal views of the city skyscrapers from both the roof terrace and from floor-to-ceiling windows inside, especially of the Empire State Building, which it directly faces.

HISTORIC HOUSES

It can surprise even lifelong New Yorkers to learn that you don't need to jump on a train at Grand Central and journey up the Hudson Valley to visit some of the most remarkable historic houses in the state. Kykuit, the Rockefeller mansion in Sleepy Hollow, and other such treasures can draw New Yorkers out of the city in the thousands, but there are a number of houses within city limits that offer the same wonderful combination of history and pastoral beauty. The two that have survived most beautifully, and which are available to hire for weddings and receptions, happen to be situated in the Bronx, a mere subway and bus ride away and yet far enough north of the busiest parts of the city to feel positively bucolic. The **Bartow-Pell Mansion** (*895 Shore Road, in the Bronx; www.bartowpellmansionmuseum.org*), in Pelham Bay Park, is both a New York City and a National Historic Landmark: an elegant mansion dating from the mid-nineteenth century, complete with a beautifully maintained classical garden and views out over Long Island Sound. Without quite being Gatsby-esque in its excess, Bartow-Pell is a breathtaking place and an almost inconceivable venue for a wedding in New York City. The mansion itself is a charming backdrop for drinking and dining, and the gardens are ideal for an outdoor reception in the warmer months. The **Van Cortlandt House** (*Broadway at West 246th Street, in the Bronx; www.historichousetrust.org/item.php?i_id=30*), tucked away in a wooded corner of Van Cortlandt Park, achieves a similarly transporting effect with very different surroundings. Built in the Georgian style, but incorporating the less formal and more rustic Dutch sensibility in its interiors, the mansion is absolutely picturesque. The house itself is comparable in size to the Bartow-Pell Mansion but arranged in a less formal way that better suits smaller parties. And while it lacks the formal majesty of the landscape at Bartow-Pell, the Van Cortlandt House has the advantage of being surrounded by parkland, making the journey there both bucolic and surreal. The total effect of being at either mansion is to be transported to a different place and time—even if that place and time is just a subway ride away from the greatest city in the world.

A SPACE WITH A CAUSE

Among the multitude of wedding venues in the city, there is a small category that operates as charitable outlets for different causes, which are supported by the venue fees you pay to rent them. The charities tend to be local outfits, which funnel the donations to their cause through a space they are affiliated with. You wouldn't know from looking at it, for instance, but on the floors above the **Prince George**

Ballroom *(15 East 27th Street, between Fifth and Madison Avenues, in Manhattan; www. commonground.org)* there are around 400 low-income apartments inhabited by formerly homeless individuals operated by the social-service organization Common Ground. The building is the former Prince George Hotel, which was once one of the largest and grandest hotels in the city (playwright Eugene O'Neill was a regular guest). As tourism declined in the 1970s, the hotel declined with it, first by taking contracts to operate as a welfare hotel, and later by being condemned and shuttered by the city. In 1996, Common Ground, an organization that rehabilitates buildings around the city to create low-income housing, acquired the building, and in addition to creating housing units, they worked to restore two of the hotel's lobby areas—the ballroom and the Ladies' Tea Room in the lobby—to their former glory. And how glorious it is! The massive Prince George Ballroom is full of opulent touches, from the bottoms of the gilded columns all the way up to the ornate carved ceiling, colored with murals of green, blue, and red, accented, of course, in gold. It's a distinctive and grand setting for a splashy wedding, but in our eyes, the real gem is the more intimate Ladies' Tea Room, which has an art deco feel, with its curved archways, elaborate carved columns, and lights set in glass cartouches. (There is a third, adjacent venue, a modern, industrial space called the World Monuments Fund Gallery, which can be rented for weddings as well.) Couples can choose among these venues or rent all three together for the ceremony, cocktail hour, and reception. One hundred percent of the venue proceeds go toward Common Grounds projects to end homelessness in New York.

Another of the city's venerable charitable institutions is Housing Works. For almost a quarter of a century, Housing Works has been working to support New Yorkers living with and affected by HIV/AIDS, and at the same time to address the ongoing crisis of homelessness in the city. Beyond the advocacy and direct services Housing Works provides, it has pioneered the approach of entrepreneurial businesses supporting a parent not-for-profit organization. This means that it creates employment, housing, and other benefits for its community by successfully running thrift stores and other businesses whose revenues feed back into support for the broader mission. The hub of the organization, therefore, also happens to be one of the city's most beloved bookstores, the **Housing Works Bookstore and Café** *(126 Crosby Street, between East Houston and Prince Streets, in Manhattan; www.housingworks. org)* in the heart of SoHo. A wonderful shop in its own right, it has become an epicenter of New York's literary scene and a favorite place for everything from high-end publishers' book launches to casual book shopping and coffee with friends. Through the Works Catering side of the organization, you can hire the space for a wedding and reception, with endless options for tailoring everything on the day from the atmosphere to the menu. The venue itself is beautiful and quintessentially SoHo: a large and open industrial space softened by the warmth of renovated details, mahogany paneling, spiral staircases up to charming balconies, and, of course, walls of books throughout. In keeping with the nature of the mission, Housing Works is available as a venue for couples and marriages of all kinds.

Couples who are interested in city preservation should consider holding their wedding at the **New Leaf Restaurant & Bar** (*1 Margaret Corbin Drive, in Manhattan; www.newleafrestaurant.com*) in Fort Tryon Park. The restaurant is run by the New York Restoration Project, a nonprofit founded by actress Bette Midler. The rehabilitation of Fort Tryon Park was one of NYRP's original missions in the 1990s; since then, the organization has expanded its mission to include a variety of efforts, all centered on the idea of making New York City cleaner and greener. Holding a wedding at New Leaf, however, is no sacrifice in the name of do-gooding. Fort Tryon Park was a gift to the city from John D. Rockefeller, who commissioned the sons and heirs of Frederick Law Olmsted to design a park on this piece of historic, scenic land overlooking the Hudson. (The cobblestone building the restaurant is housed in was envisioned as a concession stand for the park.) For history buffs, Fort Tryon is an important footprint in the city's Revolutionary-era past. It comprises the site of the Battle of Fort Washington, a decisive British victory; Margaret Corbin Drive is named for a Pennsylvania woman who manned a cannon with her husband during the battle, becoming the first woman to fight in the Revolutionary War, and the first U.S. woman to receive a military pension. (Oddly, the park still bears the name of William Tryon, who was the last British governor of New York.) For scenery mavens, the park and restaurant offer killer, quintessentially New York backdrops: there are views across the Hudson to the cliffs of the Palisades, the tree canopy of the Linden Terrace, and the famous Heather Garden, which were part of the Olmsteds' original design.

All proceeds from weddings and receptions held at New Leaf go to NYRP. You can hold both the ceremony and reception there, or have a ceremony in the park and the reception at New Leaf—though note that holding a ceremony in the park itself requires a permit from the parks department. Events can be held in the restaurant's main dining room, which can accommodate up to fifty-five seated guests, or on the patio overlooking the park. (The patio can be tented as well, if need be.)

And furthering the cause of conservation, the **Bronx Zoo** (*2300 Southern Boulevard, in the Bronx; www.bronxzoo.com*) counts among the most surprisingly picturesque venues for a wedding in the city. The zoo—which is the largest metropolitan zoo in the United States—is a treasure for many New Yorkers, and all the more beloved because it directs all the proceeds from events to the Wildlife Conservation Society. For the right kind of couple—animal lovers who want to support the zoo's presence and mission—the experience of having a part of the zoo all to yourselves is unbeatable. Whether you choose to hold your reception in the heart of the Congo Gorilla Forest among the monkeys and the mandrills, or enjoy predinner drinks in the Madagascar room with all sorts of exotic species for company, you'll feel like the zoo has been created just for you. And as anyone who has visited can attest, the architecture of the zoo's buildings is as beautiful as the conservatories of the botanical gardens across the borough, with the stonework and archways of the historic Astor Court and Beaux-Arts Zoo Center gorgeous backdrops to an outdoor ceremony, and the renovated interiors of the Schiff Family Great Hall an elegant formal dining space. And wherever you are, you're sure to be attended by several of the glamorous Indian peacocks that roam the grounds—the only things likely to be more colorful than the bouquets.

SHOPPING FOR THE BIG DAY

It's no secret that this is one of the best cities in the world for shopping, and wedding accoutrement are no exception. Whether or not you intend to be married in New York, the positioning of so many unique, world-class, and fashionable offerings in such close, walkable proximity makes this a perfect place to spend an afternoon, day, or weekend browsing for your big-day apparel and accessories. If you've ever visited New York and forced yourself to resist department stores and boutiques in favor of sightseeing and museums, this is your chance to explore a section of the city's retail largesse.

GOWN

Whether or not you are planning to tie the knot in New York, this city is rightfully a popular destination for wedding-dress shopping. Even as Pinterest and Instagram (not to mention online shopping) have revolutionized the bridal business by providing visual, searchable access to every piece of wedding paraphernalia under the sun, when it comes to the garment that is literally the focal point of this universally significant day (and which, for many women, is the one couture creation they'll ever wear), there is no substitution for the in-person, hold-it-in-your-hands shopping

A wedding dress in a Manhattan showroom

experience. New York is simply the best place in the country to find a wide range of wedding-dress purveyors in close proximity to one another (as well as, possibly, some great deals—more on that below).

The most famous wedding-dress purveyor in the city—even before *Say Yes to the Dress* parked its cameras in their dressing room—is, of course, **Kleinfeld Bridal** (*110 West 20th Street, between Sixth and Seventh Avenues, in Manhattan. www.kleinfeldbridal.com*). As millions of viewers now know, Kleinfeld is located in Manhattan, in an area that is still sometimes referred to as Ladies' Mile for the department stores that flanked Fifth and Sixth Avenues during the mid-nineteenth and early twentieth centuries. (The Ladies' Mile Historic District, which runs from Park Avenue South west to Sixth Avenue, between roughly 18th and 24th Streets, encompasses the original locations of Lord & Taylor's, B. Altman, and Bergdorf Goodman.) But before Kleinfeld took up with Manhattan in 2005 (in a move the *New York Times* described as "losing the Dodgers all over again"), the shop was in a comfortable long-term relationship with Brooklyn, where it had been a legendary bridal mecca since the '40s. Kleinfeld opened on the corner of 82nd Street and Fifth Avenue in Bay Ridge in 1941 as a fur shop but began its bridal business shortly thereafter and became known for its wide selection and personalized service. By 1968, when the store shifted exclusively to bridal wear, the out-of-the-way shop was a name whispered from bride to bride and an only-in-New-York type of destination that came to imbue its own cachet on top of whatever fitted, lace-tiered creation was selected.

Kleinfeld is no longer anything approximating a secret, and those who want their chance to be a part of this television-driven experience must be willing to brave the crowds (and sign releases). **Saks** (*611 Fifth Avenue, 5th floor, between East 49th and 50th Streets, in Manhattan. Call 212-940-2269 for an appointment; www.saksfifthavenue.com*), **Reem Acra** (*730 Fifth Avenue, Suite 205, between East 56th and 57th Streets. Call 212-308-8760 for an appointment; www.reemacra.com*), and, of course, **Vera Wang** (*991 Madison Avenue, between East 76th and 77th Streets. Call 212-628-3400 for an appointment; www.verawang. com*) are other popular venues for local and visiting brides to select their dresses. (Be aware, however, that if you are coming from out of town for a shopping trip, you must be prepared to return for fittings.) In addition, below are five lesser-known gown sources, chosen because they offer notable, more intimate alternatives to their larger, better-known counterparts. **N.B.:** All of these salons, including the ones that follow, require appointments before you visit.

Bridal Garden (*54 West 21st Street, Suite 901, between Fifth and Sixth Avenues, in Manhattan. 212-252-0661. www.bridalgarden.org. Subway: F, M to 23rd Street; N, R to 23rd*

Street) is New York's only not-for-profit bridal boutique; all proceeds from the sales of dresses from this Flatiron shop go to a charity that helps disadvantaged children. Here, you'll find new or once-worn gowns (donated by designers, stores, and brides) up to 75 percent off the retail price. The selection of gowns, sizes, and designers is constantly changing, and can include anything from independent couture lines to mainstream bridal labels such as Vera Wang, Angel Sanchez, and Lela Rose. As this is an atypical bridal boutique, visitors should expect an experience that combines vintage shopping with a bridal atelier. As at other salons, brides work with trained consultants during their appointment, who help choose gowns that will suit the bride's size and taste and advise on alterations. But instead of trying on a floor sample, brides are selecting from current offerings, and thus the experience can feel more hit-or-miss. Still, for women who like the thrill of the hunt, are looking for a bargain, or wish to bring a charitable element into the wedding-planning process, this is the place for you. And after your wedding, note that the Bridal Garden also accepts donations of designer gowns, veils, and other bridal accessories that have been purchased within the last five years.

Owner and creative director Molly Guy is on a mission to remove stuffiness and perfection from the wedding industry and replace it with high style at **Stone Fox Bride** (*611 Broadway, Suite 613B, between Houston and Bleecker Streets, in Manhattan. 212-260-8600. www.stonefoxbride.com. Subway: B, D, F, M to Broadway–Lafayette Street; 6 to Bleecker Street*). The dresses at Stone Fox (which include a house line and selections from a small number of independent designers) tend toward the bohemian, tradition-bucking side. There is minimal pouf, a number of alternatives to white (vintage block-printed silk Indian shifts stand out on the racks), and in addition to veils, Stone Fox's florist makes beautiful custom flower crowns. Instead of trying on dresses in a three-way mirror, brides emerge from a flowy, softly lit harem tent that's used as the dressing room. Attention same-sex fiancées: if you want a place where each lady can get a wedding dress that expresses her respective personal style, Stone Fox is the spot for you.

The following designer-owned boutiques carry only the named designer's label. The advantage of shopping at one of these is the personalized attention and the connection to the designer. But it's best to investigate the designers online first to make sure that their style fits with your vision of bridal.

Jussara Lee (*60 Bedford Street, between Commerce and Morton Streets, in Manhattan. 212-242-4128. www.jussaralee.com. Subway: 1 to Christopher Street; A, B, C, D, E, F, M to*

West 4th Street) is a West Village–based designer who offers truly special bespoke gowns (and men's suits as well). The collaborative design process begins with an introduction to design concepts and available materials, then progresses to more in-depth discussions about event specifics, personal style, and vision. The result is a one-of-a-kind dress and the pleasure of having had a hand in the creation of your gown. However, a bespoke gown does require a number of in-person meetings and fittings, so if you decide to go this route, be sure you can return to the city a few times before the wedding.

At the teeny-tiny NoLIta boutique **Saja** (*250 Elizabeth Street, between Prince and East Houston Streets, in Manhattan. 212-226-7570. www.sajawedding.com. Subway: N, R to Prince Street; 6 to Bleecker Street; B, D, F, M to Broadway–Lafayette Street)*, designer Yoo Lee offers ethereal bridalwear and exquisite personalized styling service. Both modern and feminine, Lee's designs are not straight-up traditional, but rather more elegant and flowy, with a touch of personality.

Elegant and exquisite—like Vera Wang with a slight indie edge—**Selia Yang**'s (*71 Franklin Street, between Church Street and Broadway, in Manhattan. 212-941-9073. www.seliayang.com. Subway: 1 to Franklin Street; 6, N, Q, R to Canal Street)* gowns are popular with stylish New York brides. (And one even made it to Hollywood, playing a supporting role in the 2008 film *Made of Honor*.) As at Saja, part of the experience of getting a gown here is working with the designer herself, who will make the extra effort to get everything right.

A Note on Sample Sales: As in other areas of fashion, New York is the location of a number of bridal sample sales and stock sales. Many of the stores and designers listed here will sell samples or leftovers from a previous year's collection at highly discounted prices, which can mean a lot when you are talking about a dress that can easily run into the thousands of dollars. If you are interested in trying your luck with these, plan ahead (most stores do sales once or twice a year, but not all places do their sales at the same time), and be prepared for some hard work. Bridal sample sales are like more emotionally fraught versions of regular sample sales, with everyone harboring the same fantasy of finding the dream dress they imagine is waiting for them somewhere on a rack. Arrive well in advance of the sale's opening time (even the less famous stores will have brides lining up hours before doors open), know what you are looking for in advance (short or long, white or ecru, lace or satin), and be prepared to make quick decisions (and possibly even throw out an elbow). It's a challenge, but finding a gown you love for hundreds rather than thousands is probably the next greatest thing after the proposal itself.

SUITS

In this age of increased informality, where Manhattan is no longer the sea of suits and hats it once was but instead must contend with overflowing tributaries of the underdressed, the requirement of men to own or indeed know how to buy a good suit has vanished. But more than any other event, a wedding is an excuse—or perhaps an opportunity—for a groom, or two grooms, or a fleet of groomsmen, to take that distinguished step toward true sartorial sophistication. As tradition would have it, a wedding is all about the dress; but as times have changed a groom's suit is once again paramount, and not merely the handsome sidekick to the bride. And just as a bride has any number of choices when it comes to gowns, a New York groom has more options now than ever before.

The best-known seller of bridal gowns in the city is also one of the institutions of menswear for weddings: **Kleinfeld** (*see page 170*). Alongside the dresses and veils in their store on West 20th Street, Kleinfeld Men also houses a smaller but reliably well-stocked groom's department, where they sell suits, tuxedos, and morning suits from most of the higher-end menswear brands (from Hugo Boss to Dolce & Gabbana, among many others). They also have a good range of formal accoutrements, from cummerbunds to top hats, and are an excellent source of advice for those in need of guidance. Sharing a spot with Kleinfeld as the most obvious choice for a groom-to-be are two major labels and chain stores: Brooks Brothers and J.Crew. At the higher end of the market, Brooks Brothers is an icon of formal menswear, and through their custom-tailoring department, they offer a range of conservative and traditional cuts of the suit and tuxedo, along with some of the best ties around. At the more accessible end of the market, J.Crew has become one of the most popular and dependable stores, not just for the grooms but also for the groomsmen: they have a succinct range of suits in more contemporary cuts, trimmer and shorter than Brooks Brothers, as well as a tailoring department that can have your groomsmen in complementary outfits for a very reasonable price.

And while getting married in New York may seem an obvious choice for some, the style of a New York wedding is everything, and there are, of course, many more unusual choices for grooms here. Some of the most prestigious high-end labels in the world have their offices in the city, and many—such as Thom Browne and Dolce & Gabbana—have special departments dedicated to tailoring for tuxedos and morning suits. There are places to find a good rental suit, to fit whatever budget and whatever time frame is required (such as the enduring institution Eisenberg & Eisenberg, in the Flatiron, where tailors on hand will be able to size you up the second you walk through the door). And the relatively recent renaissance of interest in handmade clothes, bespoke tailoring, and traditional ideas of formalwear has seen many independent tailors and smaller menswear boutiques pop up around the city in the last decade or so. So here are a few ideas for ways to dress a groom that aren't quite off the rack.

Frequently rated one of the best places to buy or rent formalwear in the city, **Baldwin Formals** (*1156 Avenue of the Americas, 2nd floor, between West 44th and 45th Streets, in Manhattan. 212-245-8190. www.nyctuxedos.com. Subway: B, D, F, M to 47th–50th Streets–Rockefeller Center*) is also just the kind of place that somebody could live in the city for years without being aware of. Hidden on a second floor above Sixth Avenue, just a needle's stitch from the Garment District, it's a no-frills purveyor of formal menswear from tuxedos to morning suits to white-tie garb, and all the accessories that go with them. The range of brands is broad enough to cover most tastes, from mainstream big labels like Hugo Boss and Calvin Klein to edgier contemporary brands such as Joseph Abboud and Ike Behar. Unlike Kleinfeld or Brooks Brothers, where the available styles are all relatively conservative, Baldwin has enough flexibility to outfit the most traditional grooms or accommodate a bit more flair, from designer vests and cummerbunds to socks and ties. And best of all, they do rentals as well.

Having started life as a small shop on Freeman Alley, **Freemans Sporting Club** (*8 Rivington Street, between Bowery and Chrystie Streets, in Manhattan. 212-673-3209. shop. freemanssportingclubcom. Subway: J to Bowery; 6 to Spring Street; F to Second Avenue*) has grown into something of a small downtown empire, with a store and a barbershop on the Lower East Side and another location in the West Village. With sharp cuts, heavy cloths, and tight fits, Freemans is increasingly the choice of the fashion-minded young man. Without explicitly specializing in wedding wear, Freemans does bespoke suits and tuxedos upon request. Working with older suppliers and very traditional methods, they make new and contemporary-looking suits the classic way, using a range of materials that errs on the conservative side. We'd recommend going with them for everything, from shoes to a haircut and shave, for the complete look.

As you'll be able to tell after only seconds in the **Lord Willy's** boutique (*225 Mott Street, between Prince and Spring Streets, in Manhattan. 212-680-8888. www.lordwillys. com. Subway: 6 to Spring Street; N, R to Prince Street*), this is a label that seeks to bring something of the traditional British taste to contemporary menswear. Besides the brighter and more mischievous designs of their regular shirts and suits, Lord Willy's also produces classic tuxedos and wedding suits with a contemporary edge, and, like a bespoke Paul Smith, is a good choice for anybody who likes a little humor hidden among their formality. (Whether that edge lies in a beautiful plaid jacket lining, a seasonal herringbone tweed for the morning suit, or a surprisingly bold bow tie is up to the groom.) Their bespoke suiting is high-end—four or five times as much as J.Crew, for example—but it's worth the expense for the big day.

INVITATIONS

An invitation is the first indication a couple can give anybody about their wedding. Before the venue and its flowers and lights, before the meal and the towering cake, before the dresses and the tears and the toasts comes the invitation. For this reason, stationers, printers, and artists all over New York have long made wedding invitations a specialty, and couples getting married in the city have given their invitations as much thought and consideration as any other element of their big day. Even with the advent of the e-vite and the increasing popularity of couples' wedding websites, the traditional printed or pressed invitation remains the gold standard for New York couples.

Among the best-known stationers in the city, Kate's Paperie is an institution of all things pretty and printed, with one store in Manhattan and an outpost in Hudson upstate. Besides being a trusted resource for off-the-rack stationery supplies, Kate's has a custom wedding-planning service that can cover anything and everything from the invitations and save-the-dates to the full package, which includes gift bags, wrapping paper for party favors, and printing for table settings and menus. Alongside Kate's, at least two other major companies compete for the attention of couples seeking the classic custom invitation. Lela New York is a high-end luxury stationer with a roster of well-known clients and a reputation for ornate work that's over the top in terms of detail and texture. Working not only with paper but also with fabrics, Lela's style is opulent and luxurious and pairs well with a traditional white wedding. On a similar scale is Ceci New York, another stationer and design firm that offers a choice between a customized ready-to-order range and a fully bespoke service. The former allows couples to delicately customize a broad range of existing designs, while the latter is among the best examples of high-end bespoke, giving couples access to a good range of papers and printing techniques.

In recent years, however, as New York has made itself one of the epicenters of a renaissance of interest in crafts and all things handmade, there are increasingly more options available to couples looking for something a little more personal or unique. Just as it is one of the fashion centers of the world, so New York is one of the capitals of American arts and crafts. Scout around and you can find a number of remarkably original stationers like the few below, which offer the opportunity to collaborate with talented artists and printmakers on save-the-dates and invitations that are as memorable and unique as everything else about your wedding.

Dempsey & Carroll (*1049 Lexington Avenue, between East 74th and 75th Streets, in Manhattan. 877-750-1878. www.dempseyandcarroll.com. Subway: 6 to 77th Street*), the venerable institution of the Upper East Side, has been in the business of printing and engraving since 1878, when it was founded with the intention not only of selling hand-engraved stationery but also of educating New Yorkers on the etiquette of correspondence. They're still equipped to do the same today, offering a fully bespoke wedding-invitation service, during consultations for which you'll be able to choose everything from paper to calligraphic style under advice from their trusted craftsmen. Their custom work is very expensive, but actual engraving is a lost art and a cut above even the finest letterpress work—it has to be seen and touched to be believed.

Among the most experienced and widely acclaimed letterpress companies in the city, **Sesame Letterpress** (*55 Washington Street, Suite 706, between Front and Water Streets, in Brooklyn. 347-768-8177. www.sesameletterpress.com. Subway: A, C to High Street; F to York Street*) has been at work in DUMBO in Brooklyn for more than a decade. All their work is done with great passion on antique pressing machines and according to the oldest rules in the letterpress book. As well as a thoroughly charming range of their own wedding designs, which can be customized to each client, they also offer a more careful bespoke service, where couples can work with the printers on every detail and at every stage of the process—including visits to the studio and, if you're lucky, a go on one of their machines. They also will print designs that are prepared by other professional designers, so if you and your loved one can have a friend design your invitations to a professional standard, all you need to do is supply the artwork and discuss the materials in the finished object with Sesame.

Beneath a carefully constructed facade of quaint Victoriana (and a pseudonym), **Mr. Boddington's Studio** (*210 West 29th Street, 9th floor, between Seventh and Eighth Avenues, in Manhattan. 212-686-5953. www.mrboddington.com. Subway: 1 to 28th Street*) is a collective of talented artists, illustrators, calligraphers, and designers who produce high-quality and whimsical stationery for any occasion. Among countless letterpress houses in the city, Mr. Boddington's Studio sets itself apart by bringing a strong sense of its own character to every piece produced, while also being open to working closely with clients on custom designs. Their range of wedding-invitation designs are given character names as if to help develop a sense of the style—the blacks and greens of the art deco–feeling Miss Royale collection, for example, contrast nicely with the cool blues and whites of the nautically themed Miss Cricket line—and are nicely pitched to be amusing without losing a sense of occasion. Set up a private appointment to discuss bespoke designs that incorporate their inimitable brand of formal whimsy for everything from invitations to table placements and gift cards.

FLOWERS

"Most people in the city rush around so, they have no time to look at a flower." So said the artist Georgia O'Keeffe, who, while living in New York in the 1920s and 1930s, had begun to make large-scale paintings of flowers as iconic as her portraits of the city's buildings. But New York also has quite a history as a flower town. Alongside the hundreds of small local florists, the bouquet-delivery chains, and the occasional deli with a good selection out front, the city even has its own neighborhood devoted to the industry. The Flower District, which now occupies just a couple of diminishing blocks on West 28th Street between the Flatiron and midtown, was for years a flourishing commercial hub, where wholesalers hoarded and displayed and ultimately distributed everything from orchids to geraniums across the five boroughs. The combination of a tightening economy and an increased reliance by larger commercial delivery companies on imported flowers has seen the district shrink in both size and influence. Although it's by no means the sole supplier to the industry these days, a few wholesalers remain there, and it's still possible to walk those blocks amid such unlikely city sights as great plastic bags of rose petals and a forest of houseplants.

Like any taste—be it for clothes, jewelry, food, wine, or potential partners for life—an appreciation for flowers is entirely subjective. It can be informed by anything and everything, from a bride's innate visual sense to a groom's memories, the sights and scents of homes and gardens past. There are countless occasions in life during which the very act of buying flowers is a gesture in itself, whose simple romance transcends such trivialities as choice of stem or palette of bouquet. But when it comes to a wedding, it's important to find a floral design that complements your and your loved one's tastes, a design that will elevate the experience and make a memorable impression on your guests.

Naturally, the range of floral designers available in New York is as varied and as colorful as a bride's bouquet. Grand, established firms with famous principal designers and celebrity clienteles compete with younger companies that have more contemporary styles. It's not particularly hard to find them—trusted local resources from the *New York Times* to *New York Magazine* keep extensive listings and publish reviews of new companies all the time—but sometimes it is difficult to know which places truly stand out and offer something the others don't. As in all fields, New York is a city where you really can go the extra mile (even when it's really only an extra block) to find something unique. So here are five floral designers who are not only up there with the very best in terms of quality and experience, but who also offer the range in style and approach that a New York couple should come to expect.

Playing on principal designer Victoria Ahn's experience as a professional dancer, **Designs by Ahn** *(208 West 30th Street, Suite 901, between Seventh and Eighth Avenues, in Manhattan. 212-929-0660. www.designsbyahn.com. Subway: 1 to 28th Street; 1, 2, 3 to 34th Street–Penn Station)* brings a theatrical approach to flowers without diminishing their intimacy. Particularly good for venues with multiple rooms, Ahn's floral arrangements are choreographed using colors and textures, creating dynamic displays that both define and respond to the mood of a space. While of course the company is open to the taste and aesthetic of every client, their style is clean and modern, and it has earned them some well-known clients in recent years. If their online portfolio isn't enough, they also have a large studio in midtown, close to the Flower District, where you can stop by to explore their range and discuss ideas in person.

With shops and offices in TriBeCa and Southampton and a quarter of a century of experience, **Élan Flowers** *(85 Franklin Street, between Broadway and Church Street, in Manhattan. 212-240-9033. www.elanflowers.com. Subway: 1 to Franklin Street; 6, N ,Q, R to Canal Street)* is in many ways the archetypal high-end New York florist. While they do offer bespoke service and work closely with clients, their aesthetic and practice is very traditional, with an emphasis on light-hued and white palettes and a kind of elegant femininity. Their byword is *classic,* and with an abundance of roses, full bouquets, and an eye for careful opulence, their arrangements are well suited to very formal weddings. They also specialize in rooftop arrangements, for those New Yorkers lucky enough to have access to one.

With a client list that includes Marc Jacobs, Ralph Lauren, and the Pierre Hotel, among others, **In Bloom New York** *(209 West 96th Street, between Broadway and Amsterdam Avenue, in Manhattan. 212-662-8852. www.inbloomnewyork.com. Subway: 1, 2, 3 to 96th Street)* is a big name in floral design. The specialty design division of Plant Shed, one of the largest florists in the city (and the only one to have its own rooftop greenhouse, so they can grow more exotic species without relying on importing), In Bloom is better suited to larger weddings. With a distinctly modern focus and a fashionable twist, In Bloom's arrangements are not necessarily the typical palette of a white wedding and lean toward a more glamorous and sophisticated look.

Founded a little more than a decade ago, with a small shop in Red Hook, Brooklyn, where they also sell handmade soaps, **Saipua** *(147 Van Dyke Street, between Van Brunt and Conover Streets, in Brookyn. 718-624-2929. www.saipua.com. Subway: F, G to Smith–9th Streets)* has evolved into a sophisticated and revered floral-design company and the cornerstone of a creative community that defines what the world has come to see as the Brooklyn aesthetic. Saipua's extraordinarily beautiful arrangements always take their inspiration from the wild, so that even the most carefully put-together bouquets have a loose and natural feel and are at once stunning and unpretentious. At World's End Farm in upstate New York, Saipua's owners cultivate their own specific visions, growing certain kinds of flowers that they can no longer find among the

A centerpiece from local florist Saipua

wholesalers of the Flower District. This way, their flowers are always seasonal and locally sourced—between their farm and other local suppliers—and their arrangements are truly unique, combining a client's taste with Saipua's distinct palette. In partnership with friend and competitor Nicolette Owen (*see below*), Saipua also runs the Little Flower School, which operates courses in flower arrangement out of its spaces in Brooklyn and at farms upstate. (Among the classes is a popular wedding workshop, so an ambitious couple can opt to take on the floral design themselves!) Their rates are high, but their work is beautiful—spend some time perusing their well-curated blogs (for Saipua and for the World's End Farm) and you'll see why this young company is the very epitome of a new kind of romance.

A child of the verdant Hudson Valley, Nicolette Owen opened her own floral design company, **Nicolette Camille** (*50 Dobbin Street, Suite 4, between Nassau and Norman Avenues, in Brooklyn. E-mail info@nicolettecamille.com for an appointment. www. nicolettecamille.com. Subway: G to Nassau Avenue*), in Greenpoint, Brooklyn, in 2006, where she would look to bring the beauty of her childhood natural surroundings to the city. A cofounder with Saipua of the Little Flower School in Brooklyn, Nicolette has quickly grown a reputation as one of the most creative floral designers in New York and has had her work published in such places as *Vogue* and the *New York Times*. The title of a book documenting her work—*Bringing Nature Home*—says everything about her style, which introduces a sense of wilderness and spontaneity to even the most formal wedding arrangements. Curated by season, Nicolette's palette is light but subtle, incorporating the pastels and dusty tones of the countryside into elegant bouquets in which pure whites or yellows shine. With this in mind, her aesthetic is best suited to a wedding with a simple or rustic feel, where her arrangements complement the atmosphere and let the bolder things—a certain dress, for example—take center stage.

REGISTRIES

Though the wedding registry was not invented here (that honor goes to Marshall Field's in Chicago), New York's esteemed retail palaces are still destinations for couples, even in a globalized shopping world. While you can now create a Tiffany's registry in countless cities around the world, you can only do so at the famed Fifth Avenue flagship when in New York.

But there are also wonderful, less mainstream places at which to create registries that, thanks again to the Internet, are accessible to guests all over the world. By registering at smaller, exclusively New York operations (such as the following), you can take a special piece of your experience in the city into your home without thoroughly inconveniencing your guests. A guest from Omaha, Nebraska, can just as easily select a chosen one of John Derian's signature decoupage plates or a piece of contemporary design from MoMA as they can pick an item from Crate & Barrel's website. Note that due to the personal nature of several of the boutiques below, appointments are suggested for couples to put together a registry.

The immense decor-and-furnishing emporium **ABC Carpet & Home** *(888 Broadway, between East 18th and 19th Streets, in Manhattan. To make a registry appointment, call 646-203-8075, or e-mail homeregistry@abchome.com. www.abchome.com. Subway: 4, 5, 6, L, N, Q, R to 14th Street–Union Square)* is a retail landmark painted with local history. Still family-owned 115 years after the founder began selling used carpets and linoleum from a cart on the Lower East Side, ABC has grown into a commanding, eight-story space on lower Broadway and evolved from its modest roots as an immigrant-owned textile purveyor into an independent, one-of-a-kind department store chic enough to be the setting for a fund-raising dinner for the Obamas. (The store's commitment to sustainability and social responsibility added to its appeal for the 2011 dinner.) ABC is a must-visit for all couples interested in global design (and you must come should you wish to register here; the store requires an in-person visit to set up a registry), as the rugs, bedding, linens, antiques, lighting, furniture, and kitchen accessories include a number of small and hard-to-find international brands and other unusual treasures. Be sure to leave yourself plenty of time to wander around selecting your items; the store is so immense and cavernous that one could imagine hiding here for ages, sleeping on demo beds covered in 600-thread-count sheets and taking meals at ABC Kitchen, the popular restaurant downstairs that serves local, seasonal cuisine, or ABC Cocina, the store's hip tapas bar. The ground floor has a pleasant bazaar of gifts, accessories, and jewelry and is a great place to pick up a surprise souvenir for your betrothed while she's looking at modernist light fixtures. Once a registry is set up, guests can purchase selections online or in the store.

"Linens are not merely linens. They are a pleasure for all of one's senses." So said Madeleine Porthault, one of the founders of **D. Porthault** *(470 Park Avenue, between East 57th and 58th Streets, in Manhattan. For an appointment, call 212-688-1660. www.dporthaultparis.com. Subway: 4, 5, 6, N, Q, R to Lexington Avenue–59th Street; N, Q, R to Fifth Avenue–59th Street)* a French couture-linen company, started in the 1920s by Madeleine and her husband, Daniel. The original venture was a lingerie boutique, but Madeleine, enchanted with impressionism and Monet's gardens at Giverny, convinced her husband to sell colorful, hand-printed sheets. At the time, this was seen as radical—it was before washing machines, and no one in the world had thought to sleep on any color aside from white—but their innovation earned their bedding (and later, linens and towels) a place in illustrious homes, including Buckingham Palace, the White House, and Élysée Palace in Paris. Their colorful, whimsical-patterned textiles were beloved by Coco Chanel, Audrey Hepburn, Jackie Onassis, and the Duke and Duchess of Windsor; one particularly romantic print, Les Coeurs, was designed for the Duke and Duchess of Windsor, based on some of the Duchess's sketches. While D. Porthault designs can be purchased at select high-end department stores across the U.S. (as well as in London, Tokyo, Cannes, and, of course, Paris), the only boutique outside of the French flagship is on Park Avenue in New York. To create a registry, couples must make an appointment to visit the store, and during the appointment the couple will work privately with one sales associate to put together a selection of items.

The small East Village shop **John Derian** (*6 and 10 East 2nd Street, between Second Avenue and Bowery, in Manhattan. For an appointment, call 212-677-3917. www.johnderian. com. Subway: 6 to Bleecker Street; F to Second Avenue*) is a bastion of uniqueness in an ever-homogenizing retail landscape, and it has an outsize reputation for its colorful and elegantly mismatched offerings. Best known for the signature glass decoupage plates made by Derian himself, the stuffed-to-the-gills shop (which is actually two separate but almost adjacent shops, separated by one storefront) also carries ceramics, furniture, floral curiosities, paintings and prints, and countless other pieces of stylish miscellany. (Don't miss the simple linocut prints by artist and sometime *New Yorker* cartoonist Hugo Guinness that endearingly depict simple subjects or urban life, like egg cartons and French bulldogs.) The look is classy but eclectic, the kind of things you dream of finding at a Paris flea market—or in a rich spinster aunt's attic. As at D. Porthault, registries must be curated at the store in person; guests can purchase items by visiting or calling the store and requesting the list. Items are gift-wrapped and shipped from the New York store.

The Museum of Modern Art is one of the city's top museums, and its design shop, known as the **MoMA Design Store** (*11 West 53rd Street, between Fifth and Sixth Avenues, in Manhattan. 212-708-9700. www.momastore.org. Subway: F, M to Fifth Avenue– 53rd Street; 81 Spring Street at Crosby Street in Manhattan. Subway: 6 to Spring Street*), is a destination in its own right. The store is an extension of the museum's mission to promote and exemplify good design from around the world. Every item in the store is approved by one of MoMA's curators; some items are designed by artists whose works are in the museum's design collection, while others are designed exclusively for the museum. (Both Manhattan stores feature special store-within-stores for Muji, the cult Japanese minimalist lifestyle brand.) The stores are filled with clever kitchen and dining equipment, stylish housewares, and many unique gadgets that solve the pesky problem of form and function, all of which can be added to a wedding registry online or in the store. (Guests who are MoMA members get their standard member's discount.) There are plenty of great ideas in the modest to moderate price points; however, if you and your spouse-to-be are serious cooks and want to go all out, consider registering for the gorgeous Malle W. Trousseau, a 43-piece set of beautifully designed kitchen equipment from around the world, inspired by the pieces Trousseau's daughter wanted to take for her kitchen when she left home. **N.B.:** The MoMA Store has two locations by the museum, as well as a SoHo outpost.

Maxwell-Silver New York *(Call 212-799-1711 or e-mail registry@maxwellsilverny. com to set up a registry. www.maxwellsilverny.com.)* isn't a destination in itself but rather a clever service that lets you register for some of New York City's signature unique offerings in a way that's easy and accessible for guests all around the world. Maxwell Silver is a group registry with gift items from a curated selection of small boutiques, museums, and local designers. Say, for instance, you're taken with Alexandra Ferguson's YES, DEAR pillow and a set of Shabbat candles from the Jewish Museum. Neither Ferguson nor the museum has its own registry, but by setting up an online registry with Maxwell-Silver, you can make these gifts a reality, along with china, housewares, and wine from Manhattan's Burgundy Wine Company. It's an excellent way to bring a bit of the city's special feeling to wherever your home is; though keep in mind that because most of the retailers on the site are small or independent, the return policy is not as liberal as larger stores.

CHAPTER 6

THE MARRIAGE INDEX

Every year, between 70,000 and 100,000 marriages take place in New York City. Our city presents countless options for venues—from grand and iconic to intimate and off-the-beaten path—making it a popular choice for local couples, those planning destination weddings, and, since 2011, same-sex couples. Luckily, the city's recent investment in the Marriage Bureau at the Manhattan City Clerk's Office has made the experience of getting legal marital paperwork together more pleasant and less byzantine, and resulted in a glitzy renovation of the Manhattan marriage chapel to make a wedding at City Hall a destination affair. Whether you're hosting your dream wedding celebration here, or are just beginning to research the protocol after the question is popped, this section is for you. It's an alphabetical, by-the-letter list of everything you need to know to be married smoothly, legally, and happily in New York City. More than just a list of rules and requirements, it's also a guide that can help you and your loved one tie the knot in the greatest city on earth.

A

Appointment: You don't need an appointment to get a marriage license or to be married at City Hall. All marriage business is handled by the City Clerk's Office on a first-come-first-served basis. Exceptions to this policy are extremely rare and are granted only when the disruption a couple would incite because of crowds, police presence, or paparazzi would prevent the bureau from functioning properly. (Notable exemptions include the wedding of Mel Brooks and Anne Bancroft, and the 2005 wedding of Matt Damon and Luciana Bozan Barroso.)

Attire: Most people don't dress up to file for a marriage license. However, if you will be returning to City Hall a day (or more) later to get married, anything goes. Expect to see gowns, jeans, suits, saris, and maybe even a themed costume or two (especially if it's Halloween)—a manner of dress that's as eclectic as the people themselves.

B

Blood test: New York doesn't require one! Couples can proceed directly to the City Clerk's Office.

Britney Spears Rule: New York has a so-called "Britney Spears rule," otherwise known as a waiting period. Your marriage cannot take place less than one day after you pick up a marriage license, unless you are granted a judicial waiver.

C

City Clerk's Office: The New York City Marriage Bureau is part of the City Clerk's Office, one of the oldest offices in city government and one that dates back to the city's time as a Dutch colony. If you're going to be married in New York City, you'll need to go to a branch of the City Clerk's Office (there's one in each borough) to obtain your license. And regardless of whether you're getting married at the Manhattan City Clerk's Office (better known as "getting married at City Hall") or another locale in the city, remember that, per the "Britney Spears rule," you will have to wait twenty-four hours after applying for your license to hold the ceremony.

Here are the addresses of the City Clerk's Offices:

- *Manhattan City Clerk's Office: 141 Worth Street, between Leonard and Centre Streets, in Manhattan. www.cityclerk.nyc.gov. Subway: 4, 5, 6 to Brooklyn Bridge City Hall; R to City Hall; 2, 3 to Park Place; A, C to Chambers Street.*
- *Bronx City Clerk's Office: Supreme Court Building, 851 Grand Concourse, Room B131, between East 158th and East 161st Streets, in the Bronx. www.cityclerk.nyc.gov. Subway: 4, B, D to 161st Street-Yankee Stadium.*
- *Brooklyn City Clerk's Office: Brooklyn Municipal Building, 210 Joralemon Street, Room 205, between Court Street and Boerum Place, in Brooklyn. www.cityclerk.nyc.gov. Subway: 2, 3, 4, 5 to Borough Hall; R to Court Street.*
- *Queens City Clerk's Office: Borough Hall Building, 120-55 Queens Boulevard, Ground Floor, Room G-100, between Union Turnpike and 82nd Avenue, in Queens. www.cityclerk. nyc.gov. Subway: E, F to Kew Gardens Union Turnpike.*
- *Staten Island City Clerk's Office: Borough Hall Building, 10 Richmond Terrace, Room 311, at the intersection of Hyatt Street and Stuyvesant Place (across the street from the ferry terminal), on Staten Island. www.cityclerk.nyc.gov.*

Comfort: The Marriage Bureau in Manhattan moved into a new, renovated office in 2009 as part of an effort to position New York City as an international marriage destination. And for the home to a branch of city government, it's surprisingly plush. In the new building, you enter a central rotunda, where there are computer terminals you use to sign in and fill out any paperwork that you haven't completed online. Once you've signed in, you'll receive a number, and then you and your party can kick up your heels and admire the setting until your number is called. The fluorescent lighting, cracked floors, and the electric chapel sign that had seen brighter days have been replaced by chandeliers, 1930s-era marble tables (which hail from the building's earlier incarnation as the office of the Department of Motor Vehicles), art deco crown moldings, and bronze countertops. The bathrooms even have full-length vanity mirrors for outfit checks and touch-ups. The ceremonies are performed in two non-denominational "chapels," each decorated in a different color scheme: one in peach and apricot hues, the other in purple and lavender.

D

Domestic Partnership: A domestic partnership is a legal expression of a committed non-marriage relationship that extends some of the benefits of marriage to partners who choose not to be married. Formerly the closest legal alternative to marriage for same-sex couples, domestic partnerships are still popular with committed couples who are not ready to or do not wish to be married. Domestic partners can partake in some of the benefits of marriage—including succession, property rights, and medical dictates— without all of the restrictions (and protections) of a legal marriage. The process to register for domestic partnership is similar to the one for getting married: you can apply online or in person at the City Clerk's Office, and both members of the couple must appear in person to complete the registration. The fee ($35) and ID requirements are the same. The city clerk can perform a domestic partnership ceremony (like a wedding, it is $25), though a witness is not required. Domestic partnerships that are registered in New York City are only available to couples in which at least one partner lives in or is employed by New York City. Information about the process, requirements, and benefits offered (and not offered) with domestic partnerships is available in the Marriage Bureau section of the City Clerk's Office website (*www.cityclerk.nyc.gov/html/marriage/marriage_bureau.shtml*).

E

Entourage: Parents, friends, kids, photographers, and make-up artists, can all join the party—there's no limit. If you are eloping on your own, remember that you will need at least one witness to sign the marriage license.

Errors (on a Certificate of Marriage Registration): Don't let day-of jitters get the best of you. Keep cool—and have both spouses proofread the certificate of marriage registration, because making corrections is a hassle. Correcting information such as birthdates or spelling of names requires submitting a notarized form, and either mailing a photocopy of your identification as proof or bringing it back to the City Clerk's Office. (If you are submitting your application by mail and are sending photocopies of ID documents, your amendment application must include a notarized statement that the notary has viewed the original documents.) Changes are free for up to twenty-four hours following the ceremony if you are married at the clerk's office, or up to two weeks if you are married elsewhere; after that, they charge $10. And make sure you are comfortable with your choices on name changes: name changes (and changes back) are not considered amendments, so if you change your mind about your new surname, you and your spouse must reapply for a marriage license and get married again.

F

Fees: The fee for a marriage license is $35. It can be paid by credit card or money order. The fee for a marriage ceremony at the City Clerk's Office is $25.

G

Gifts: Believe it or not, there's a gift shop at the City Clerk's Office, an outpost of the CityStore (*a856-citystore.nyc.gov*), the official gift shop of New York City. In addition to "Married in New York" mugs, ornaments, T-shirts, and bumper stickers, it also sells big-day essentials like flowers, veils, garters, hairspray, tissues, clip-on bow ties, and Champagne flutes.

H

Hours and Holidays: Marriages run long; the Marriage Bureau does not. Offices are open from Monday through Friday from 8:30 a.m. to 3:45 p.m. in Manhattan and the Bronx; the branches in Brooklyn, Queens, and Staten Island are open until 4:00 p.m. The offices are all closed on U.S. legal holidays (the same as postal holidays), including New Year's Day, Martin Luther King Jr. Day, Presidents' Day, Memorial Day, Independence Day, Labor Day, Columbus Day, Election Day, Veterans Day, Thanksgiving, and Christmas. The clerk's office is open on some non-legal observances—when Valentine's Day and Halloween fall on weekdays, they are usually among the busiest days of the year.

I

ID: You'll need it both to pick up the marriage registration and to get through security in the building. Passports, driver's licenses, non-driver IDs, military IDs, and certificates of naturalization or permanent resident cards are all valid, so long as they are not expired. Your witness must have ID as well.

J

Judicial Waiver: It's possible to bypass the twenty-four-hour waiting period (otherwise known as the "Britney Spears rule") by procuring a judicial waiver after receiving a marriage license. A judge can grant a judicial waiver, which allows a couple to marry immediately, after hearing the pair plead their extenuating circumstances. In Manhattan, the judge's office is across the street from the Marriage Bureau.

K

Kiss the Bride (and Kiss Her Again!): There's no prohibition against being married twice, once at City Hall and later at a venue of your choosing. Many couples—local and visiting—choose to have their official ceremonies at City Clerk's Offices and their "social weddings" elsewhere, thus relieving their officiants of the burden of sending back the marriage license. If you decide to change your surname after the marriage license is filled out, you will be legally required to remarry your spouse.

L

License: A license from the State of New York is required to be married in New York City, whether or not you are holding your ceremony at the Marriage Bureau in a City Clerk's Office. The application can be completed online, but it must be picked up by both members of the couple. A marriage license issued in New York may be used anywhere in the state (including any of the five boroughs), but is not valid for out-of-state or out-of-country weddings. The license is good for 60 days (or 180 days for active military personnel).

M

Marriage Bureau: This is the division of the City Clerk's Office where licenses are provided, marriages are performed, and records are kept. There is one Marriage Bureau in each borough.

Minute: One minute is the length of a typical ceremony performed by a judge at City Hall. (Consider that each judge averages seventy to eighty weddings a day, except Fridays, when the number is even higher!)

N

Name Changes: In New York State, either or both members of a couple may change their last name (or names) upon marriage. For couples that decide to change their names, there are four options: the surname of either spouse; any former surname of either spouse; a name combining into a single, unhyphenated surname the complete or partial pre-marriage surname of each spouse (or any former surname of either spouse); a hyphenated surname combining the complete pre-marriage surnames of both spouses (or any former surname of each spouse). New York State does not mandate any name changes, and couples do not need to have the same surname. However, only a surname can be changed via a marriage license; if you wish to change your surname officially and make your pre-marriage surname your middle name, the change of your middle name must be processed separately. Changes to surnames after the certificate of marriage registration is issued (other than the correction of errors in the spelling of the name itself) are not considered amendments; the only way to change the name on your certificate of marriage registration is to be married again (really!).

Number: When you arrive at City Hall for a wedding, you'll sign in at a computerized kiosk and be given a ticket with your wedding number on it. You and your betrothed will wait in the lobby until your number is called out on an illuminated screen. No one collects the ticket at the end, so hold on to it—it's the most unique New York City wedding souvenir there is!

O

Ordination: The easiest way for a layperson to become eligible to perform a marriage ceremony is to be ordained as a minister. While this is by no means to be taken lightly, and of course is only a viable option for those whose beliefs and principles allow, it's the most convenient way for people who wish to be married by somebody they know to do so—since few of us know the mayor (*see Who*). Institutions like the Universal Life Church offer quick services that are tailored to the city's unique requirements.

P

Photography: If you're getting married at City Hall, you're welcome to bring along a photographer, whether a friend or a hire—but note that once inside you will be required to move through the ceremony as directed by city officials, which means there isn't much time during the ceremony or immediately afterward for photographs (*see Minute*). Also note that there are a couple of local legends who position themselves around City Hall specifically for the purposes of offering themselves as both witnesses and photographers, should arriving couples be in need of either or both.

Previous Marriages: Under New York State law, anybody wishing to be married must provide information regarding any and all previous marriages.

Q

Queue: Waiting in line at the Marriage Bureau is a part of the process, but it's a lot more pleasant here than at other places of local bureaucracy. After you get your number, you'll file into a beautiful waiting room with marble floors and touches of art deco style in the fixtures and furnishings and join what's likely to be the liveliest and most excited queue of your life. There are people of all kinds (*see Xenophilia*), each of whom is waiting with a mixture of happiness and nerves for the big moment. This is one line you won't mind getting in.

R

Records: The City Clerk's Office holds records of all marriages from 1930 to the present day, and these can be requested by mail, online, or in person at any time. Romantics with local roots can pull copies of relatives' certificates, whether to give as gifts or for their own inspiration—and what's more New York than having your union kept on record, downtown in the heart of the city's oldest neighborhood, for future New Yorkers to see? Fees start at $15 for a copy of a record, and can go up to $35 or so depending on the type of certificate you'd like and the legal purpose of its use.

Registration (Certificate of Marriage): The certificate of marriage registration is the document that is mailed to you after the ceremony and becomes your legal proof of the marriage. (This is different from the marriage license, which is the document you must apply for in-person at the City Clerk's Office, which your officiant will give or mail back to the office for its records after the ceremony has been performed.)

S

Same-Sex Marriage: Since the Marriage Equality Act was signed into law in 2011, same-sex couples can legally be married in New York. When it comes to ceremonies at City Hall or other civic ceremonies, the rules and regulations for everything from licenses to officiants remain the same, whether the spouses-to-be are of the same or opposite sex.

Summer Fridays: The busiest days of the year for City Hall weddings. A colorful, bustling marriage bureau certainly lends a distinct shade of romance, but if you think a long wait to kiss the bride will kill the romance—or if you've got a reception to make elsewhere—avoid Fridays from May to September. (Tip: Tuesday is the least busy day of the week.)

T

Timing: Though queues for City Hall weddings have been much streamlined since the Marriage Bureau's 2009 renovation, some times of day are still busier than others. First thing in the morning is typically the least busy, followed by the end of the day. If you want space and speed, avoid the midday lunch rush. As a general rule, allow at least 90 minutes from arrival to "I do."

Toast: Celebrate your marriage with food and drink from one of the fine establishments within a dress-heeled walk of the Clerk's office. At City Hall Restaurant *(131 Duane Street, between West Broadway and Church Street, in Manhattan; www.cityhallny. com)*, just a few blocks from the offices, an old–New York feel and art deco–accented interiors set the stage for a classic steak menu. Blaue Gans *(139 Duane Street, between West Broadway and Church Street, in Manhattan; kg-ny.com/blaue-gans)* is the TriBeCa outpost of chef Kurt Gutenbrenner's small empire of Austrian restaurants, with a broad menu of simple but rich mittel-European dishes and a fine list of crisp complementary wines. Also on Duane Street is celebrity chef David Bouley's eponymous flagship restaurant, Bouley Restaurant *(163 Duane Street, between Hudson Street and West Broadway, in Manhattan; www.davidbouley.com/bouley-main)* famed for its exquisite tasting menus and private dining rooms of various sizes and characters. (Do be sure to reserve in advance, especially if you're interested in a private room.) The Peking Duck House *(28 Mott Street, between Pell and Mosco Streets, in Manhattan; www. pekingduckhousenyc.com)* is the ritziest restaurant in Chinatown. Elegantly served crispy duck is the house specialty, and the restaurant's formal white linens have served as the backdrop for many smaller downtown receptions. Also, the Odeon (*145 West Broadway, between Thomas and Duane Streets, in Manhattan; www.theodeon-restaurant.com*) is one of the enduring French restaurants of lower Manhattan, ideal for Champagne and cocktails at the more relaxed bar before a reliably delicious bistro dinner.

U

Usher: When you are married at the City Clerk's Office, you're welcome to invite whomever you like to be part of your wedding party, as long as you remember to operate within the time constraints of the ceremony (*see Minute*). It's common for couples to invite only small groups of guests to witness the ceremony, but some decide to designate an usher to lend formality to the occasion, and to introduce a buffer between the officials of City Hall and the wedding party itself.

V

Vows: If you get married at City Hall, the standard procedure is for the officiant to read the simplest and most traditional marriage vows, asking each member of the couple to take the other as his or her bride or groom, and to live together in marriage "for better or worse, richer or poorer, in sickness and in health . . . ." You're welcome to write your own vows to read at the ceremony, but be aware that you must let the officiant know at least two days in advance of the ceremony if you intend to do so, and note that time is limited for each service—so you may want to save the longer professions of love for the reception!

W

Websites: Information, addresses, hours, and requirements are all available on the Marriage Bureau page of the City Clerk's Office website: *www.cityclerk.nyc.gov/html/marriage/marriage_bureau.shtml*. There is also an online form that couples can fill out in advance that will speed up the registration process for the marriage license.

Weekends: Saturday and Sunday may be great days for a party, but plan to get your paperwork together during normal working hours. The City Clerk's Office is open only Monday through Friday, which means you can't pick up a marriage license or have a wedding at City Hall over the weekend. A visiting couple can make a holiday out of their wedding by arriving in New York in time to get the license on a Friday and being married the following Monday.

Who: In addition to ordained members of the clergy and ministers of any religion (*see Ordination*), New York State also allows a number of state-elected officials, including county clerks, local judges, and present and former mayors of the city to be marriage officiants. The person planning to perform the marriage needs to register as an officiant, with identification affirming his or her position as one of the above, with the Manhattan City Clerk's Office.

Witness: At least one (adult and ID-carrying) witness must be present at any wedding in New York. (A blood relative is okay.)

X

Xenophilia: As is true for most things in New York City, getting married at the clerk's office in City Hall is a study in xenophilia. This is a place for people of all kinds, ages, and persuasions who may have arrived in New York City for any number of reasons. The only thing everybody here has in common is a desire for the union of marriage, and that communal emotion can provide an experience unlike any other. So be prepared to share your big day, and maybe even forge new friendships with strangers once you have this experience in common.

Y

Yes (or Sí, Oui, Da, Ja ...): While ceremonies at the City Clerk's Office can be conducted only in English or Spanish, it's very easy to find officiants for civil ceremonies anywhere else in the city who can conduct marriages in other languages. Once you've identified your ideal location, check the most up-to-date local listings (such as those on *nymag.com*, which regularly updates its listings of registered officiants) and you should be able to say yes to a ceremony in just about any language you like. The City Clerk's Office also offers a telephone translation service that can interpret the required legal forms into 170 different languages.

Z

Zoos (and an Aquarium!): Though they're smaller than their counterpart in the Bronx (*see page 167*), the zoos in Central Park, Prospect Park, and Flushing Meadows all offer unique environments for ceremonies. And once restoration is complete in 2015, following damage incurred due to Hurricane Sandy, the New York Aquarium at Coney Island will once again be available for those who have always dreamed of a ceremony bathed in dappled blue light.

INDEX

BOROUGH INDEX

ACKNOWLEDGMENTS

This book was a labor of love many years in the making. We are extremely thankful for the patience, good faith, and editorial wisdom of Kathleen Jayes; we're grateful for a working relationship that has now spanned ten happy years. The inspiration for this book came from our publisher, Charles Miers, whose commitment to presenting an unironically beautiful New York to our readers—a rare thing these days—set the tone for our research. Thanks as well to Susi Oberhelman for this lovely design, Mina Pekovic for picture research, and our beloved Kayleigh Jankowski for making the proposal-spot map.

Our own ideas and experiences of romance were hardly enough to fill a book, and much of our inspiration came from real stories of courtship and marriage from our friends and family. Thank you Lauren Aronoff-Jensen, Simon Bird, Giulia Di Filippo, Carolina Dorson Ponzer, Abigail Kagle, Charlotte Kaiser Weinberg, Martha Kaiser, Lusiné Kerobyan, Dana Kugelman, Niko Triantafillou, Jennifer Wu, Michelle Wu, and Joy Yoon for sharing your stories, pictures, and ideas.

Finally, thank you to our respective romantic partners, Alex Ostroy and Joana Kelly, for being our supporters and occasional guinea pigs of our (sometimes great, sometimes totally misguided) ideas about romance in New York.

C&J

PHOTO CREDITS

Images on the following pages are copyright © Shutterstock / the respective photographers:
7 Alan Kraft; 9 KJ2495; 16 gary718; 19, 22 Sean Pavone; 26 Colin D. Young; 32 f11photo;
54, 101 Robert Crum; 58 Stuart Monk; 85 Ben Bryant; 88 T photography; 97 ErickN;
119 Jack Aiello; 122 Manuel Hurtado; 132 KAZMAT; 136 Dee Golden; 139 David W. Leindecker;
143 Songquan Deng; 153 Elzbieta Sekowska; 161 Jeff Williams; 169 Lev Radin

Other photographs by page number: 25 © Demetrio Carrasco / JAI / Corbis;
46, 80, 108 photographs by Alexandra Rowley; 51 © Christophe Launay / Aurora Photos / Corbis;
150 © APlights / Design Pics / Corbis; 179 © Sarah Ryhanen / Saipua

Postcards on the following pages are courtesy of the Museum of the City of New York:
2–3, Columbus Circle and Central Park, ca. 1940; 4–5, Skyline of Downtown New York as seen
from Brooklyn at Night, ca. 1940; 10, Walk Under Bridge, Prospect Park, Brooklyn, ca. 1910;
12–13, Brooklyn Bridge, New York City, ca. 1937; 38–39, Central Park seen from Rockefeller Center,
ca. 1945; 76–77, Terraces in Central Park, ca. 1910; 112–113, Riverside Drive, George Washington
Bridge and Hudson River at Night, ca. 1940; 144–145, Central Park at 59th Street, showing
the hotels Plaza, Savoy-Plaza-Sherry Netherlands, and Pierre at Night, ca. 1940; 184–185,
Midtown Skyline looking toward East River, ca. 1940; 196, Public Library, 5th Avenue and 42nd
Street, New York City, ca. 1936; 206, Chrysler Building at Night, New York City, ca. 1940

Proposal map design page 148 by Kayleigh Jankowski

First published in the United States of America in 2015
by Rizzoli Ex Libris, an imprint of
Rizzoli International Publications, Inc.
300 Park Avenue South • New York, NY 10010 • www.rizzoliusa.com

© 2015 Caitlin Leffel and Jacob Lehman

2015 2016 2017 2018 / 10 9 8 7 6 5 4 3 2 1

Distributed in the U.S. trade by Random House, New York

Printed in China

ISBN-13: 978-0-7893-2751-2

Library of Congress Catalog Control Number: 2014940845